A Management Guide
to PERT / CPM

JEROME D. WIEST

Associate Professor of Management Science
Rice University

FERDINAND K. LEVY

Professor of Economics
Rice University

PRENTICE-HALL, INC., *Englewood Cliffs, New Jersey*

FOR YVONNE AND MIMI

© 1969
by Prentice-Hall, Inc.
Englewood Cliffs, New Jersey

13–548511–8
LIBRARY OF CONGRESS CATALOG CARD NO: 71–78802
CURRENT PRINTING (last digit)
19   18   17   16   15

PRENTICE-HALL INTERNATIONAL, INC., *London*
PRENTICE-HALL OF AUSTRALIA, PTY. LTD., *Sydney*
PRENTICE-HALL OF CANADA, LTD., *Toronto*
PRENTICE-HALL OF INDIA PRIVATE LTD., *New Delhi*
PRENTICE-HALL OF JAPAN, INC., *Tokyo*

Printed in the United States of America

Preface

This book has two purposes. First it is intended to acquaint the student in management-oriented courses with all the fundamental concepts necessary to understand and use PERT and CPM scheduling techniques. Second and equally as important, the book is designed as a guide and a basic reference to these techniques for both potential and actual users in industry. It seems timely to provide a small guide to PERT/CPM scheduling and control methods that is compact but complete in its coverage.

The emphasis throughout the book is on the basic ideas of these techniques and the variety of management problems to which they may be applied. More advanced methods, especially mathematical ones, using the PERT/CPM techniques and computer programs, are fully discussed in the appropriate appendices to the chapters. Small exercises, with their solutions, designed to make sure that the reader fully understands the fundamentals of PERT and CPM, are at the end of the book. These exercises are keyed by chapters so that a concept introduced in a particular chapter has a problem that uses it in the exercises.

The literature on PERT and CPM has become voluminous. We have tried to present a bibliography at the end of the book which, although not complete, is comprehensive in its coverage of concepts and the myriad of applications of these techniques. An understanding of the ideas presented in this book should be sufficient background for anyone wanting to read further in this growing area.

The idea to write this book was born while we were both graduate students at Carnegie Institute of Technology, collaborating on a series of research papers introducing and developing these techniques. We gratefully acknowledge the support given us there by the Graduate School of Industrial Administration and later by Rice University that enabled us to complete the book. Our thanks go to Professor William R. King of the University of Pittsburgh for his helpful suggestions. We also want to thank *Operations Research* and the *Harvard Business Review* for granting us permission to include material originally presented in those journals in this book. Finally, we express our deepest appreciation to Mrs. Betty Banner for her excellent typing of the final manuscript and to Miss Betty Neville of Prentice-Hall, Inc., for her painstaking editing of it.

JEROME D. WIEST
FERDINAND K. LEVY

Contents

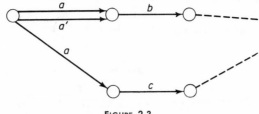

FIGURE 2-3

identical; hence they will have the same alternate job identifications. Since we wish to assign unique names to jobs, we need a device to eliminate this complication in drawing the arrow diagram.

To overcome these difficulties, we introduce the concept of a *dummy job*, or *dummy activity*. A *dummy job* takes zero time to perform and is used solely to illustrate precedence relationship when the use of actual jobs only would lead to the complications outlined above. To illustrate how a dummy job is used, let us return to the budget example. Let f be a dummy activity whose immediate predecessor is job a, and let b have a' and f as immediate predecessors. The arrow diagram of the budget project can then be drawn as in Figure 2–4, with the dummy job indicated by a dashed-line arrow.

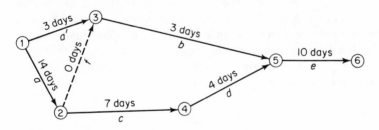

FIGURE 2-4. Arrow Diagram of W-L's Revised Budgeting Project

Notice in Figure 2–4 how the dummy job f is used: a and a' are both immediate predecessors of b. Since a supposedly is an immediate predecessor of dummy activity f, and f is an immediate predecessor of b, then a is no longer an immediate predecessor of b, but is still a predecessor. That is, a still has to be done before b can be started, because it is an immediate predecessor of the dummy f which must be completed before b can be begun. Also, we are now able to show a as an immediate predecessor of c without showing a' as one, which of course it is not. However, a' is shown as an immediate predecessor of b, and, moreover, all jobs are shown by only one arrow. Thus, the addition of dummy jobs eliminates the difficulty encountered when two or more activities have some, but not all, of their immediate predecessors in common. The information on the jobs in Figure 2–4 and their new alternate symbols are shown in Table 2–3.

TABLE 2-3

The Project of Budgeting (Revised)
With Dummy Jobs for Drawing the Arrow Diagram
W-L Company

Job Identification	Alternate	Job Description	Immediate Predecessors	Depart- ment	Time to Perform Job
a	(1,2)	Forecasting Unit Sales	—	Sales	14 days
a'	(1,3)	Surveying Competitive Pricing	—	Sales	3 days
f	(2,3)	Dummy Activity	a	—	0 days
b	(3,5)	Pricing Sales	a', f	Sales	3 days
c	(2,4)	Preparing Production Schedules	a	Production	7 days
d	(4,5)	Costing the Production	c	Accounting	4 days
e	(5,6)	Preparing the Budget	b, d	Treasurer	10 days

A good question to ask at this point is, How do we recognize when the arrow diagram of a project will require dummy jobs? As stated above, there is a need for dummy activities when the project contains groups of two or more jobs which have some, but not all, of their immediate predecessors in common. A simple way to add dummy jobs is to let all the common immediate predecessors of two or more jobs lead into a single node and then let the dummies emanate from this node. We illustrate this with an example of a small project. Suppose we have the jobs in the project given in Table 2–4 with their immediate predecessors.

TABLE 2-4

Job List—Project I

Job Identification	Immediate Predecessors
a	—
b	—
c	—
d	a, b
e	b, c

Activity b is a common immediate predecessor of both d and e; while a is an immediate predecessor of d alone, and c is one of e. We then let b lead into two dummy jobs f and g, and let f be an immediate predecessor of d, and g be one of e as shown in Figure 2–5.

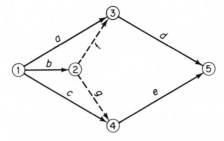

FIGURE 2-5. Arrow Diagram—Project I

By adding jobs to Table 2–4 along with the alternate names for all the jobs, we produce Table 2–5.

TABLE 2-5

Job List With Dummy Jobs—Project I

Job Identification	Alternate	Immediate Predecessors
a	(1,3)	—
b	(1,2)	—
c	(1,4)	—
f (dummy)	(2,3)	b
g (dummy)	(2,4)	b
d	(3,5)	a, f
e	(4,5)	c, g

A more complicated example of project requiring dummy jobs is given in Table 2–6. Jobs *d, e,* and *f* have *a* as a common immediate predecessor,

TABLE 2-6

Job List—Project II

Job Identification	Immediate Predecessors
a	—
b	—
c	—
d	a, b
e	a, c
f	a, b, c

while they have some combination of *b* and *c* as one also. The arrow diagram

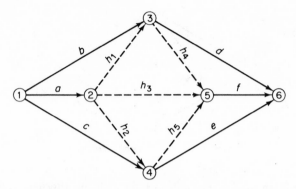

FIGURE 2-6. Arrow Diagram—Project II

for that project with the dummies indicated by h_1 to h_5 is shown in Figure 2-6.

Notice that job f has dummies h_3, h_4, and h_5 for immediate predecessors; these in turn have a, b, and c as immediate predecessors, which really means that f's predecessors are a, b, and c as indicated in Table 2-6. Similarly h_1 and h_2 substitute for a as immediate predecessors of d and e respectively. The complete table of jobs for this project is illustrated in Table 2-7.

TABLE 2-7

Job List with Dummy Jobs—Project II

Job Identification	Alternate	Immediate Predecessors
a	(1,2)	—
b	(1,3)	—
c	(1,4)	—
h_1	(2,3)	a
h_2	(2,4)	a
h_3	(2,5)	a
h_4	(3,5)	b, h_1
h_5	(4,5)	c, h_2
d	(3,6)	b, h_1
e	(4,6)	c, h_2
f	(5,6)	$h_3, h_4. h_5$

Again, note in the above table that if a job is an immediate predecessor of another activity, the terminal node of the predecessor must be identical with the initial node of its immediate successor.

The Activity-on-Node Diagram

The addition of dummy jobs to an arrow diagram is a cumbersome procedure, and, moreover, it adds items to the table of jobs and enlarges the graph. As we shall see in the next chapter, the calculations which are necessary to perform critical path or PERT scheduling make use of all jobs, actual and dummy, and hence are lengthened as dummy jobs are added.

A second type of project graph, or network, called the *activity-on-node diagram*, or graph, has been devised to overcome the foregoing objections to the arrow diagram. The activity-on-node graph, which we shall abbreviate by AON, is constructed so that the jobs are denoted by circles, or nodes, and the immediate predecessor relationship between two jobs is shown by an arrow connecting the two nodes. The arrow's point, of course, is at the successor's *node*. Thus, if job *a* is an *immediate predecessor* of job *b*, we portray this relationship on the AON graph as shown in Figure 2–7.

FIGURE 2-7. Two-Activity Example—AON Diagram

These two jobs graphed on an arrow diagram would look like Figure 2–8.

FIGURE 2-8. Two-Activity Example—Arrow Diagram

For a more complicated example showing how dummy jobs are not needed in an AON graph see W-L's revised budgeting project in Table 2–2 (page 8) worked out in Figure 2–9.

Note the ease with which the AON diagram can be drawn. Just draw a circle for each job and then connect each to its immediate successor with a directed arrow. The identifications, or names, for a job and the amount of time required to complete a job is usually inserted in the job node. Also AON graphs usually contain fictitious nodes labeled "start" and "finish," so that there will be a unique beginning and end to the graph of the project. For example, if there were no "start" node in Figure 2–9, it would be difficult to tell whether the project began with job *a* or job *a'*. Figure 2–10 illustrates

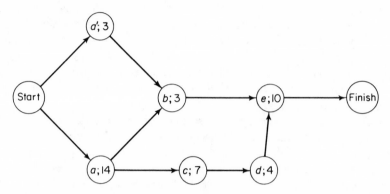

FIGURE 2-9. AON Diagram—The Project of Budgeting (Revised) W-L Company

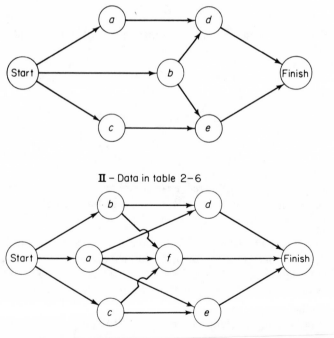

FIGURE 2-10. AON Diagrams—Small Projects I and II

the use of the AON graph with the data given in Table 2–4 (page 10) and Table 2–6 (page 11).

It seems that an AON diagram is much simpler to draw than an arrow diagram, and hence a good query is, Why should we bother with the arrow diagram at all? The truth of the matter is that, even though both are used, the arrow diagram is by far the more prevalent, primarily because it was used first and became firmly established. The emphasis in the PERT model on "events," which we shall describe in Chapter 4, reinforced the use of arrow diagrams in which *nodes* refer to events. That is, the completion of several activities culminating at a node is referred to as an event, or milestone. At this point new decisions can be made, schedules reevaluated, and so on. And finally, some prefer to use the arrow diagram because it is more suggestive of work-flow associated with activities than are nodes or circle representations.

As we shall see in succeeding chapters, the calculations necessary to do PERT and CPM scheduling make use of the immediate predecessor and successor relationships among jobs in a project. If a computer is used to perform these computations, the arrow diagram portrayal of a project permits us to use much less storage in the computer than the AON diagram. This is because job identifications with the arrow diagram show the predecessor and successor relationships automatically. If a job is an immediate predecessor of another, its terminal node is the initial node of the successor. On the other hand, using the AON graph forces us to list each job's immediate predecessors or successors along with the job, which requires a significant amount of space.

Thus, as can be seen, both types of project graphs have their shortcomings. Yet, because of its better adaptation to PERT procedures, the arrow diagram continues to be in more widespread use today than the corresponding activity-on-node graph. We now turn to an illustration of both in a housing construction example.

Example—Building a House[2]

A simple and familiar example should help to clarify the process of drawing a project graph. The project of building a house can be readily analyzed by critical path and PERT techniques. While a contractor might want a more detailed analysis, we shall be satisfied here with the major *jobs*, together with their times and their immediate predecessors shown in Table 2–8. In the table asterisks indicate where dummy jobs may be needed in

[2]This example is derived from a similar one in "The ABC's of the Critical Path Method" by J. D. Wiest, F. K. Levy, and G. L. Thompson in the *Harvard Business Review*, Sept.-Oct., 1963.

drawing an arrow diagram.[3] Since the AON diagram can be drawn directly from the table, it is given first as Figure 2–11.

TABLE 2-8

House Construction Project

Job Name	Description	Immediate Predecessors	Time (days)
a	Excavate, Pour Footers	—	4
b	Pour Concrete Foundations	a	2
c	Erect Frame and Roof	b	4
d*	Lay Brickwork	c	6
e	Install Drains	b	1
f	Pour Basement Floor	e	2
g	Install Rough Plumbing	e	3
h*	Install Rough Wiring	c	2
i*	Install Air Conditioning	c, f	4
j	Fasten Plaster and Plaster Board	g, h, i	10
k	Lay Finished Flooring	j	3
l**	Install Kitchen Equipment	k	1
m**	Install Finished Plumbing	k	2
n	Finish Carpentry	k	3
o	Finish Roofing and Flashing	d	2
p	Fasten Gutters and Downspouts	o	1
q	Lay Storm Drains	b	1
r*	Sand and Varnish Floors	n, s	2
s	Paint	l, m	3
t*	Finish Electrical Work	s	1
u	Finish Grading	p, q	2
v	Pour Walks, and Landscape	u	5

Table 2–9 again lists the jobs in the home construction project but with alternate job names and dummy jobs inserted as necessary to aid in drawing the arrow diagram which follows in Figure 2–12.

Note in the arrow diagram that dummy job D_2 was needed because jobs l and m had k as an identical immediate predecessor, giving them the same initial node, and they also had the same immediate successor s, which gave them both the same terminal node. Thus, they would have had identical node numbers, that is, both would have been (10, 12) and would have become indistinguishable had we not inserted the dummy job D_2 as a substitute for k the immediate predecessor of activity m.

[3]Those jobs with a single asterisk have some, but not all, their immediate predecessors in common. Those with a double asterisk have identical immediate predecessors and successors.

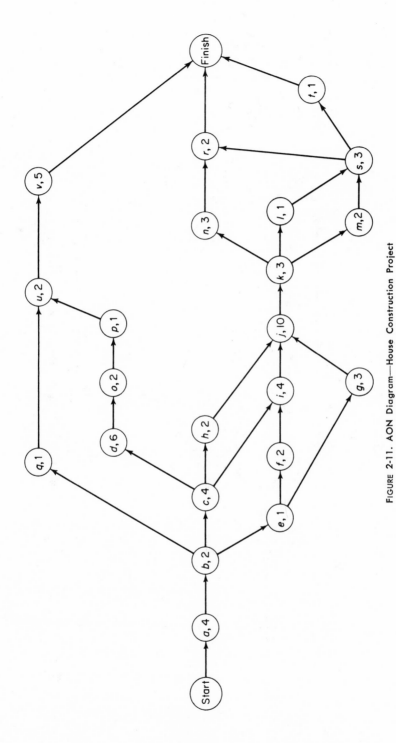

FIGURE 2-11. AON Diagram—House Construction Project

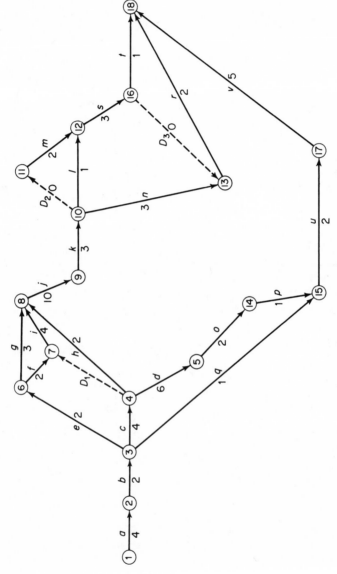

FIGURE 2-12. Arrow Diagram—House Construction Project

TABLE 2-9

House Construction Project

Job Name	Alternate	Immediate Predecessor	Time (days)
a	(1,2)	—	4
b	(2,3)	a	2
c	(3,4)	b	4
d	(4,5)	c	6
e	(3,6)	b	1
f	(6,7)	e	2
g	(6,8)	e	3
h	(4,8)	c	2
D_1 (dummy)	(4,7)	c	0
i	(7,8)	D_1, f	4
j	(8,9)	g, h, i	10
k	(9,10)	j	3
l	(10,12)	k	1
D_2 (dummy)	(10,11)	k	0
m	(11,12)	D_2	2
n	(10,13)	k	3
o	(5,14)	d	2
p	(14,15)	o	1
q	(3,15)	b	1
D_3 (dummy)	(13,16)	s	0
r	(13,18)	D_3, n	2
s	(12,16)	l, m	3
t	(16,18)	s	1
u	(15,17)	p, q	2
v	(17,18)	u	5

Network Scheduling—A Summary

This chapter developed the concept of breaking down a *project* into *activities* in order to draw its *graph*, or *network*. This decomposition is necessary for performing the basic calculations necessary to do PERT or critical path scheduling. Before proceeding to show how these calculations are performed, we shall quickly review the terminology and ideas developed in the present chapter.

A *project* is said to consist of a collection of independent *activities*, or *jobs*. If one job has to be completed before another can begin, we say the first job is an *immediate predecessor* of the job following or equivalently, the latter is an *immediate successor* of the former. This predecessor relation among jobs can be shown by a *project graph*, or *network*.

Two types of graphs were illustrated. The *arrow diagram* shows the jobs as *arrows* connecting two *nodes*, or circles, and the immediate predecessor relationship between two jobs is denoted by the predecessor's *terminal (ending) node* being identical with its successor's *initial node*. Reasons for adding *dummy jobs*, that is, jobs requiring zero time for completion, were also given. It was shown that dummy jobs are needed in constructing an arrow diagram if two or more activities in the project have *identical* immediate predecessors and successors, or if two or more jobs have *some, but not all*, of their immediate predecessors in common. A second type of graph, called the *activity-on-node graph*, was illustrated. In the *AON diagram*, jobs are portrayed by nodes and the immediate predecessor relation between two jobs by an arrow from the node representing the predecessor to the node representing the successor.

3

Finding the critical path

Once we reduce a project to a network of activities and events and we estimate activity durations, we are in a position to determine the minimum time required for completion of the whole project. To do so, we must find the *longest path*, or sequence of connected activities, through the network. This is called the *critical path* of the network, and its *length* determines the duration of the project. In this chapter we are primarily concerned with finding and measuring the critical path in a project network. First of all, however, we must clearly define what we mean by a *path* in a network and by the *length* of a path. We hope to accomplish this with the aid of the following simple example.

Suppose the W-L Company has two salesmen who meet for dinner one night in San Francisco. They discover that they are both going to Los Angeles the next day and agree to continue their conversation at dinner that night. The first salesman, whom we shall call Mr. Allen, lives in Santa Barbara and plans to go through that city, have lunch with his wife, and then travel on to Los Angeles. Mr. Baker, the other salesman, has an appointment with a customer for lunch in Bakersfield and must go there on the way to Los Angeles. As both have to work in Los Angeles the day after they arrive, they want to meet for dinner as early as possible. Their problem then is to decide the earliest possible time to meet for dinner if they both leave at 8 : 00 A.M. the next morning.

The driving time from San Francisco is about eight hours if one goes through Bakersfield on U.S. 99 and about eleven hours if one goes through Santa Barbara on U.S. 101. This is shown on Figure 3–1. The driving time in hours is shown adjacent to the arrows indicating the

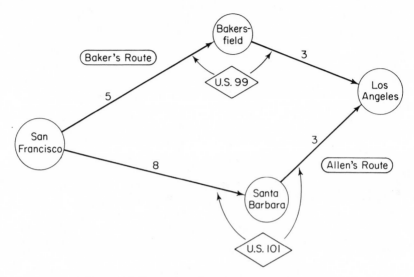

FIGURE 3-1. Routes from San Francisco to Los Angeles

direction of travel. (Note the similarity between Figure 3-1 and the arrow diagrams of Chapter 2.) Moreover, if we assume that both Mr. Allen and Mr. Baker will spend two hours for lunch respectively, then we can describe their travel to Los Angeles as a project, whose final event is their meeting for dinner. The project's activities with their immediate predecessors are given in Table 3-1, and the project's arrow diagram is portrayed in Figure 3-2.

In order to determine the earliest Allen and Baker can meet for dinner, we must find out which one will take longer to reach Los Angeles. From Figure 3-2 it is obvious that Mr. Allen will take 13 hours (8 from San

TABLE 3-1

Project of Traveling to Los Angeles

Job Name	Alternate	Job Description	Immediate Predecessors	Time (hours)
a	(1,2)	Allen drives from San Francisco to Santa Barbara	—	8
b	(2,3)	Allen lunches with wife	a	2
c	(3,6)	Allen drives from Santa Barbara to Los Angeles	b	3
d	(1,4)	Baker drives from San Francisco to Bakersfield	—	5
e	(4,5)	Baker lunches with customer	d	2
f	(5,6)	Baker drives from Bakersfield to Los Angeles	e	3

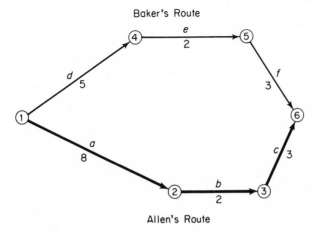

Baker's Route

Allen's Route

FIGURE 3-2. Arrow Diagram of Project of Traveling to Los Angeles

Francisco to Santa Barbara, 2 for lunch in Santa Barbara, and 3 from Santa Barbara to Los Angeles), while Baker will need only 10 hours to reach Los Angeles. Thus, if both leave San Francisco at 8 : 00 A.M., the earliest dinner appointment they can make is 9 : 00 P.M. (8 : 00 A.M. + 13 hours).

Notice how we made the above calculation. We found Allen's time to reach Los Angeles by beginning at node 1 and seeing how long it took him to reach node 2; then we added this time (8 hours) to the time it took him to reach node 3. Finally, we took this sum and added the time between node 3 and node 6. Similarly, we obtained Baker's time for travel by adding the times between nodes 1 and 4, 4 and 5, and 5 and 6.

On this network there are two ways to start at beginning node 1 and traverse the network to ending node 6. These two ways are called *paths*. A *path* is a set of nodes connected by arrows, which begin at the *initial node* of a network and end at the *terminal node*. In Figure 3–2 there are two paths, 1–2–3–6 and 1–4–5–6, where the numbers refer to the nodes. The *length* of a path in a network is the total time it takes to travel the path. This time is calculated by adding the individual times between connected nodes on the path.

A path is called a *critical path* if it is the longest path in a project network. Thus, Allen's path, which we have drawn in bold face, is the only critical path in the project of traveling to Los Angeles. Activities, or jobs, on critical paths are referred to as *critical jobs*, or *critical activities*. These jobs are critical in determining the project's duration: To shorten the time to complete a project, we must shorten the jobs on the longest path in its network —the critical path.

To see this, note that if Mr. Baker decides to eliminate his stopover in Bakersfield, activity (4, 5), thus shortening his travel time to 8 hours, it *still* takes 13 hours before he and Mr. Allen can meet in Los Angeles. On the other hand, if Allen cuts his lunch time in Santa Barbara from 2 hours to 1, then they can meet in 12 rather than 13 hours. Again, Mr. Allen's path and the jobs along it are *critical* in determining the length of the project, that is, when he and Baker can meet in Los Angeles.

As a further exercise in finding paths and their lengths in an arrow diagram, consider the project shown in Figure 3–3.

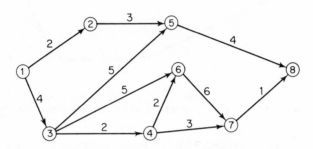

FIGURE 3-3. Example Arrow Diagram

If you list all possible sequences from start to finish, you will discover that there are *five* distinct paths in the network, namely:

> A. 1–2–5–8,
>
> B. 1–3–5–8,
>
> C. 1–3–6–7–8,
>
> D. 1–3–4–6–7–8,
>
> E. 1–3–4–7–8.

From the activity duration given alongside each arrow in Figure 3–3, you should be able to verify that C (1–3–6–7–8), is the critical path, with a length of 16.[1]

Thus far we have been using an *arrow diagram* to illustrate the calculation of a project's critical path. The calculation is computed in the same manner for an AON diagram. The only difference is that the activity times we add are given at the *nodes* in this graph rather than along the *arrows* as in the arrow diagram. We will draw an AON diagram, Figure 3–4, using the Allen-Baker trip example of Table 3–1.

The paths in the figure are: (1) Start-*a-b-c*-Finish and (2) Start-*d-e-f*-Finish.

---

[1]The path lengths are 9(A), 13(B), 16(C), 15(D), and 10(E).

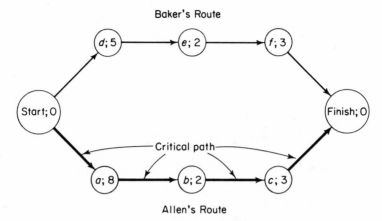

Baker's Route

Allen's Route

FIGURE 3-4. AON Network of Project of Traveling to Los Angeles

The lengths of the paths, computed by adding the time at each node, are $0 + 8 + 2 + 3 + 0 = 13$ hours and $0 + 5 + 2 + 3 + 0 = 10$ hours, respectively. The critical path is (1) since it is longer than (2).

Multiple Critical Paths

We stated earlier that the only way to shorten a project is by reducing the time needed to perform one or more critical activities, that is, jobs on the critical path. However, a project may have more than one critical path. For example, if Baker took five hours for his luncheon appointment rather than two, it would take thirteen hours for him to reach Los Angeles; both paths would then be critical. In order for Baker to meet Allen sooner, *both* would have to shorten the time used for their trips. In general, if there are two *independent* critical paths (that is, critical paths with no jobs in common), then at least *two* activities (one on each path) must be shortened to reduce the project length. If the paths share one or more jobs in common, then shortening one of the common jobs will simultaneously shorten both critical paths and hence the project itself. The same considerations hold if there are multiple critical paths. All must be shortened simultaneously if project duration is to be reduced.

As an example in point, consider the project shown in Figure 3–5. Note that all paths are 15 time units long. There are many ways of shortening this project, but to do so at least one—and perhaps as many as five— jobs must be shortened. To cite a few examples, one could reduce project duration by shortening:

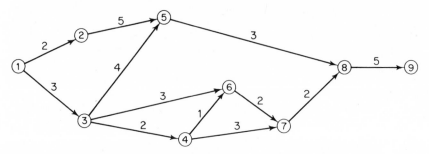

FIGURE 3-5. Arrow Diagram of Project with Multiple Critical Paths

   a. job (8, 9)
   b. or jobs (1, 2) and (1, 3)
   c. or jobs (5, 8), (6, 7), and (4, 7)
   d. or jobs (1, 2), (3, 5), (3, 6), and (3, 4)
   e. or jobs (2, 5), (3, 5), (3, 6), (4, 6), and (4, 7)[2]

In Chapter 5 we shall discuss how to find the best combination of jobs to shorten, but for now we just observe that alternative ways for reducing project length usually exist.

Job Slack

Going back to our original example where Allen's path is critical, we note that Baker can leave three hours later than Allen and still not delay their dinner. Alternatively, Baker could travel more slowly or take longer for lunch in Bakersfield, as long as the total delay did not exceed three hours. We say then that Baker has some *slack* in his path, or more generally speaking, that jobs not on the critical path have slack (relative to critical jobs). Such information is extremely useful to project managers because it tells them how much flexibility they have in scheduling various jobs. But before learning how job slack may be calculated, let's first consider an efficient method for finding which jobs are critical.

An Algorithm for Finding the Critical Path

In the previous section we showed how jobs not on the critical path could be delayed or lengthened without changing the time needed to com-

[2]Such combinations of jobs may be found by taking "cuts" of the network, in which a line is drawn through the network, from above to below, always cutting through arrows oriented counterclockwise to the direction of the cut line. The above examples represent five of fifteen possible cuts in the network shown.

plete the project. In this section we devise a set of procedures that will identify the critical path and which will show how the start and finish times of certain activities may be changed without affecting the duration of the project. In general, a set of procedures or collection of rules specifying calculations which lead to a desired result is referred to as an *algorithm*. Hence we shall present an algorithm for finding the critical path of a project and the start and finish times of all the activities within the project.

For purposes of exposition, we shall use the budget example of Chapter 2. Its arrow diagram is reproduced in Figure 3–6. Recall that a job's name is given above the arrow and its duration below. We shall describe shortly what the brackets above and below the arrows denote.

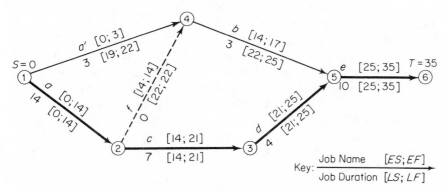

FIGURE 3-6. Arrow Diagram of W-L's Revised Budgeting Project

Early Start and Early Finish Times

We begin with some definitions. The *early start* of a job in a project is the earliest possible time that the job can begin, and we label it $ES(\ )$, where the job name appears in the parentheses. Thus we denote the early start of job a in Figure 3–6 as either $ES(a)$ or $ES(1,2)$. The *early finish* of a job, denoted by $EF(\ )$, is its early start time plus the *time* needed to complete the job. For job a this would be $EF(a) = ES(a) + t(a)$.

Now, before a job can start, all of its immediate predecessors must have been completed. Suppose the project of budgeting at W-L begins at time 0. Since jobs a and a' have no predecessors, then $ES(a)$ is 0 and $ES(a')$ is 0 and their corresponding early finish times are $EF(a) = 0 + 14 = 14$ and $EF(a') = 0 + 3 = 3$. In general, we indicate the *start time* of a project by the symbol S. For jobs with no predecessors, then $ES = S$. In all examples throughout this book we will set $S = 0$, but S could just as well be a calendar date.[3]

Once again the early start time of jobs a and a' in our budgeting example is 0, the start time of the project, since both have no predecessors. Now let's look at job c. It cannot start until its immediate predecessor a is completed; hence its earliest start $ES(c)$ is a's earliest finish time, or 14. Job c's early finish time is its early start time plus the time needed to complete it, or $EF(c) = ES(c) + t(c) = 14 + 7 = 21$. Similarly, job f, a dummy activity, can be started only when its immediate predecessor a is completed; thus $ES(f) = 14$. Since f is a dummy job, its duration is zero and hence $EF(f) = 14$.

Early start and early finish times are recorded on Figure 3–6 within the brackets *above* the arrows. The number before the semicolon in the brackets is the early start time, the number following is the early finish time. In symbols, we denote early start and finish times by $[ES, EF]$.

Thus far we have calculated ES and EF for jobs a, a', c, and f. Note that we *cannot* yet calculate these times for job e. Why? Because we do not yet know when its predecessors will be completed. Specifically, we have not calculated early finish times for b and d. Let's do so for job b.

Job b cannot be started until both a' and f are completed. The early finish time of a' is 3 and that of f is 14. Since *both* have to be completed before b begins, b cannot begin until day 14. So we write $ES(b) = 14$. In general, the *early start time* of a job is the largest, or maximum, of the early finish times of *all* of its immediate predecessors.

Job d's early start time is 21, the early finish time of c, its only predecessor. It follows that $EF(d) = 21 + 4 = 25$ and $EF(b) = 14 + 3 = 17$. Now we can calculate $ES(e)$ as the maximum of the EF times of b and d, its immediate predecessors. Since 25 is the maximum, then $ES(e) = 25$ and $EF(e) = 35$. Thus the budget can be completed in 35 days. We usually refer to the completion, or finish date, as T, so $T = 35$ in our example.

Obviously, if the earliest completion date of the budget is 35 days after its beginning, the longest path through its network must be 35 days in length. A fast perusal of Figure 3–6 will show this to be correct; the path consisting of jobs a, c, d, and e is 35 days long. This sequence, then, is the project's *critical path*—the longest path in the network.

To briefly summarize our procedure, we start at the beginning of the project network and calculate the early start and then the early finish times for each of the beginning jobs (those with no predecessors). Then we do the same for their successors, their successors' successors, and so on until all jobs in the project have been considered. This procedure is called the *forward*

---

[3]Naturally, if calendar dates are used, then the calculations described here have to be "calendarized" to account for changes in months, days not worked, and so on. Thus, in the above example if S is January 20 then $EF(a) = 20 + 14 = 34$ or February 3, assuming all days are worked.

pass through the network. Notice that no job can be considered until all of its immediate predecessors have been. Thus the jobs are examined in *technological order*. (A list of jobs from a project is in technological order if no job appears in the list until all of its predecessors have been listed.[4]) The forward pass, then, yields an *ES* and *EF* for each activity, and the earliest finish date, *T*, for the project.

Late Start and Late Finish Times

As we mentioned before, activities which are not on the critical path can be delayed without delaying the completion date (*T*) of the project. Reasonable questions are, *How much* can they be delayed? How *late* can a particular activity be started and still not lengthen the project's duration? It will be helpful in answering these questions if first we define the *late start* (*LS*) of an activity as the latest time it can begin without pushing the finish date of the project further into the future. Similarly, the *late finish* (*LF*) of an activity is its late start time plus its duration. In symbols for job *a*, $LF(a) = LS(a) + t(a)$, or, in a form which will be more useful, $LS(a) = LF(a) - t(a)$.

To calculate late start and late finish times, we begin at the end of the network and work backwards. This time we go through a *backward pass*. In our budget example, that means that we start at node 6. The only job leading into node 6 is job *e*. It must be completed by day 35 so as not to delay the project; therefore, day 35 is its late finish. In general, for jobs with no successors, we set $LF = T$.

Since it takes 10 days to do job *e*, it must begin at day $35 - 10$ or day 25, which is its late start. Now there are two jobs, *b* and *d*, which are predecessors of *e*. The *LF* times of both have to be 25, or *e* would be delayed beyond its *LS* and the project not completed by day 35. Then *b*'s late start is 22, since $LS(b) = LF(b) - t(b) = 25 - 3 = 22$. Similarly, *d*'s late start is 21, since the job has a duration of 4 days. Note that we have recorded the late start and late finish times for jobs just below their arrows in Figure 3–6. They are written as [*LS*; *LF*].

Job *c* is the only activity leading into node 3, and its *LF* becomes 21 since that is the *LS* of *c*'s lone successor, job *d*, which emanates from the node. Subtracting *c*'s duration of 7 days, we obtain $LS(c) = 21 - 7 = 14$. Two jobs lead into node 4, *a'* and *f*. Their *LF* must be 22, the *LS* of job *b* emanating from the node. Thus $LS(a') = LF(a') - t(a') = 22 - 3 = 19$, and $LS(f) = 22 - 0 = 22$.

There are two jobs, *f* and *c*, which begin at node 2. $LS(f)$ is 22 and

---

[4]Usually, there is not a single technological ordering but several possible ones. Thus, in our example job *b* could come before or after *c* in the list, as long as *a*, *a'*, and *f* appear before either of them.

$LS(c)$ is 14; so the late finish time of any job leading *into* this node must be the smallest, or the minimum, of the late starts of the jobs beginning at the node. Hence $LF(a)$ is 14, the minimum of 14 and 22. $LS(a)$ then equals $LF(a)$ — $t(a)$ or $14 - 14 = 0$. So *a* must begin at day 0. We have completed our backward pass, which yielded late start and finish times for all jobs. This information is quite useful, as we shall see below.

Total Slack

Looking at Figure 3–6, we observe that for some of the jobs, *late starts* and *early starts* (or similarly, *late* and *early finishes*) are identical. Thus $ES(a) = LS(a) = 0$ and $EF(d) = LF(d) = 25$. On the other hand, for example, $ES(b)$ is 14 and $LS(b)$ is 22. This means that job *b* may start any time between day 14 and day 22 and still not delay the completion of the project. We say then that job *b* has *slack*, and we define the *total slack* (*TS*) of a job, or activity, as the difference between its late start and early start times (or equivalently, as the difference between its late finish and early finish times). For job *b*, we have

$$TS(b) = LS(b) - ES(b) = 22 - 14 = 8 \text{ days}$$

or

$$TS(b) = LF(b) - EF(b) = 25 - 17 = 8 \text{ days}$$

Obviously, if a job is on the critical, or longest, path, delaying its start would delay the project finish date. Hence its late and early start times must be identical. A quick glance at Figure 3–6 will show this to be true. It follows that jobs on the critical path have *zero* total slack, for if their $LS = ES$, then the difference between the two must be zero. Another definition of a critical path, therefore, is one whose jobs have zero total slack.

If we delay the start of a noncritical job (one which has *slack*), we shall frequently delay the start of the jobs succeeding it. For example, suppose we delay job a' until day 18. Then its *EF* time is $18 + 3 = 21$. If job *f* is completed by day 14 as before, *b* still cannot be started until day 21, the completion date of a'. Thus *b*'s *ES* increases from 14 to 21, and its total slack is reduced from 8 days to 1 day $(22 - 21)$. We should be aware that use of the total slack of a job by delaying it will often affect the total slack of succeeding jobs.

Free Slack

However, such is not always the case. For instance, in our budget example notice that the early start time of *b* is 14, To put it another way, *b* cannot start until job f is completed on day 14. Job a' is also a *predecessor* of b, but a' takes only 3 days to complete. Thus, it can start as late as day 11 and still *not* delay the early start of b. We say then that a' has *free slack* (*FS*), which we define as the amount of time a job can be delayed without affecting the early start time of any other job. For calculation purposes, the *free slack* of a job is the difference between its early finish time and the earliest of the early start times of all of its immediate successors. Thus $FS(a') = ES(b) - EF(a') = 14 - 3 = 11$. Free slack, of course, can never exceed total slack;[5] moreover, all jobs that have total slack do not necessarily have free slack. Witness job f where $TS(f) = 22 - 14 = 8$ days but $FS(f) = ES(b) - EF(f) = 14 - 14 = 0$. The only other job with free slack in our example is b which has $FS(b) = 8$. In general, a job has free slack if it has more total slack than one of its immediate successors.[6]

Both free slack and total slack have useful managerial interpretations, but total slack is probably the more widely used of the two. Throughout this book, when we refer to slack we will mean to *total* slack, unless we note otherwise. In the next section we shall have more to say about the important concept of slack and about its use.

Use of the AON diagram instead of the arrow diagram does not change any of the above procedures. To calculate the ES for a job, one must still examine the EF of all predecessors; and the job's LF is determined from the LS of its successors. EF, LS, TS, and FS are calculated as before. The resulting data is recorded by the job *nodes* of the AON diagram, rather than on the arrows.

To summarize the critical path algorithm, jobs in a network are first listed in technological order. Then the following calculations are performed for each job in a *forward pass* through the list (from top to bottom);

S = start time for project (usually = 0)
$ES(a) = S$ for all beginning jobs, or
$ES(a) = \max\{EF \text{ (all predecessors of } a)\}$
$EF(a) = ES(a) + t(a)$
$T = \max\{EF \text{ (all jobs)}\}$ = earliest finish time for project.

Then in the *backward pass* up through the job list, the following are calculated:

$LF(a) = T$ for all ending jobs, or
$LF(a) = \min\{LS \text{ (all successors of } a)\}$
$LS(a) = LF(a) - t(a)$
$TS(a) = LS(a) - ES(a) = LF(a) - EF(a)$
$FS(a) = \min\{ES \text{ (all of immediate successors of } a)\} - EF(a)$.

---

[5] An exception to this observation is noted in the next section.
[6] Another method of calculating free slack for a job is to determine the difference between its total slack and the *minimum* total slack of all its immediate successors.

Project Due Dates Which Differ from Earliest Completion Time

In the backward pass procedure, we based our calculations on T, the earliest time that the project could be completed as determined by using the forward pass procedure. Implicitly, we assumed that T represented the *desirable* completion date or target date or due date of the project. Such is not always the case, however. Project planners may wish to establish a target date that permits more slack in the schedule to allow for unforeseen problems or to increase flexibility in allocating resources to jobs. On the other hand, it is also possible that a due date earlier than T may be imposed externally—for example, by the Defense Department on a contractor for a missile project. Pressure would then be on the contractor to find ways of shortening the project duration, or he would face the possible payment of overtime penalties.

These possibilities may easily be incorporated in the critical path algorithm. Instead of setting the late finish times of all ending jobs equal to T, we set them equal to the *desired* project due date, say, D. Backward pass calculations proceed exactly as before, but some of our previous conclusions would have to be modified.

Note that if the due date D is later than the earliest possible completion time T, then all activities in the project will have slack—including those on the critical path. For example, assume that the W-L Budgeting Project in Figure 3–6 has a target date of 40 days. Since its longest path is 35 days, all jobs on this path have 5 days of slack. Any one of them could be delayed up to 5 days without extending the project finish date beyond the target date of 40. In fact, *every* job in the project has 5 more days of slack than our previous calculations showed.[7] While we can still define the critical path as the longest sequence of jobs in the network, it is no longer true that critical jobs are slackless. But it is true that no job has less slack than critical jobs.

To generalize these observations, if we base calculations in the backward pass on an assumed project due date D, then all jobs will have D minus T more units of slack than they would if the calculations of LS and LF were based on the earliest project completion date T. Thus all critical jobs will have $D - T$ units of slack. If $D = T$, then critical path jobs will be slackless, as before. If D is greater than T, critical path jobs will have positive slack.

What happens, however, if D is less than T: if the due date is earlier than the minimum project completion date? The same analysis holds as above, but since $D - T$ is now negative, some jobs—possibly all of them,

[7] We are talking here about total slack, of course. Free slack is unaffected by a change in target date because free slack is based only on a job's early start and finish times, which are independent of the project target date.

but at least the critical path jobs—will have *negative* slack.[8] Critical jobs will have exactly $D - T$ units of slack, the least amount of any jobs. If a project manager sees negative slack figures on project jobs, he knows that one or more of these will have to be expedited or the project probably will not be completed by the due date.

A Digression on Slack

When a job has zero total slack, its scheduled start time is automatically fixed (that is, $ES = LS$), and to delay the calculated start time is to delay the whole project. Jobs with positive total slack, however, allow the scheduler some discretion in setting their start times. This flexibility can be usefully applied to smoothing work schedules. Peak loads that develop in a particular shop—or on a machine, or within an engineering design group, to cite other examples—may be relieved by shifting jobs occurring on peak days to their late starts. Slack allows this kind of juggling without affecting project time.[9]

Free slack can also be used effectively at the operating level. For example, if a job has free slack, the foreman may be given some flexibility in deciding when to start the job. Even if he delays the start by an amount equal to or less than the free slack, the delay will not affect the start times or slack of succeeding jobs (which is not true of jobs that have no free slack). For an illustration of these notions, we return to our house-building example.

Back to the Contractor

In Figure 3–7 we reproduce the AON diagram of a house-building project, marking the *ES* and *EF* above and the *LS* and *LF* below each job— for example, 0; 4 are above and 3; 7 are below the *a*; 4 circle. We assume that construction begins on day zero and must be completed by day 37. Total slack for each job is not marked. Remember it is the difference between the numbers representing *LS* and *ES* and those representing *LF* and *EF*. However, jobs that have positive free slack are so marked. There is one critical path, which is shown by heavier lines in the diagram. All critical jobs on this path have total slack of 3 days.

Several observations can immediately be drawn from the diagram: (1) The contractor could postpone starting the house for 3 days and

---

[8]Since free slack is unaffected by D, then if $D - T$ is negative, it is possible that a job's free slack may exceed its total slack, an exception to the general observation made in an earlier section. We should have said, $TS \geq FS$ (TS is greater than or equal to FS) as long as $D \geq T$.

[9]Chapter 7 presents a full explanation of this idea.

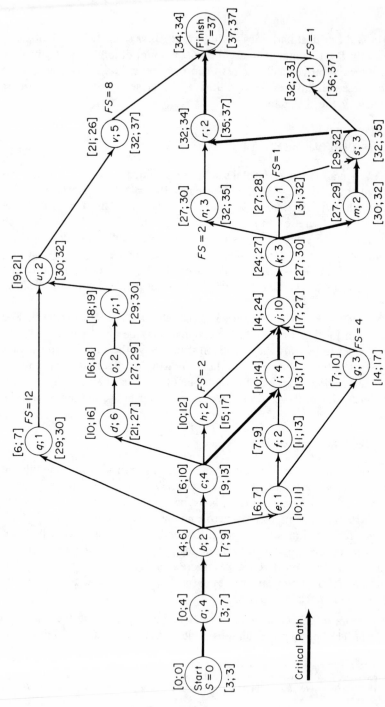

FIGURE 3-7. AON Diagram of House-Building Example

34

still complete it on schedule, barring unforeseen difficulties (see the difference between early and late times at the finish). This would reduce the total slack of all jobs by 3 days, and hence reduce *TS* for critical jobs to zero.

(2) Several jobs have free slack. Thus the contractor could delay the completion of *h* by 2 days, *f* by 1 day, *g* by 4 days, *q* by 12 days, and so on—without affecting succeeding jobs.

(3) The series of jobs *d*, *o*, *p*, *u*, and *v* have a comfortable amount of total slack, 11 days. The contractor can use these and other slack jobs as "fill in" jobs for workers who become available when their skills are not needed for currently critical jobs. This is a simple application of work-load smoothing: juggling those jobs with slack in order to reduce peak demands for certain skilled workers or machines.

If the contractor were to effect changes in one or more of the critical jobs, by contrast, the calculations would have to be performed again. This he can easily do, but in large projects with complex sequence relationships, hand calculations are considerably more difficult and liable to error. Computer programs have been developed, however, for calculating *ES*, *LS*, *EF*, *LF*, *TS*, and *FS* for each job in a project, given the set of immediate predecessors and the time required for each job. An example of such programs is given in the Appendix to Chapter 4.

4

The PERT model

Both CPM and PERT, as we have noted, use the project network. It is the basis of both techniques, and the notions of critical paths and activity slack are common to each. How then do they differ? Why two models? For historical reasons mainly. The models were developed independently and in somewhat distinct problem settings. As it has turned out in actual applications of the two models, some of their differences have disappeared or at least have become less important. But, traditionally, each has had a special emphasis of its own—each has been concerned with somewhat different aspects of the scheduling problem. Perhaps this is because they were originally applied in different kinds of industries and to somewhat different kinds of problems.

The Problem of Uncertainty

PERT was developed for and has been used most frequently in the aerospace industries—notably in research and development types of programs. These industries are relatively new; their technology is rapidly changing, and their products are nonstandard. CPM, on the other hand, has most frequently been applied to construction projects. For the most part, houses, bridges, and skyscrapers use standard materials whose properties are well known. They employ long-developed and well-seasoned components, and they are based on a more or less stable technology. Changes occur mainly in design—sizes, shapes, and arrangements—rather than in design concepts.

By contrast, while there is some standard hardware in ICBMs and lunar rockets, much of their design and construction requires new developments in materials and technology, and projects are contracted, planned, and scheduled before all technological problems have been solved. All of this is to say that there is a large amount of uncertainty in the development of new weapons systems and space ships—uncertainty about the times required for developmental research, engineering design, and ultimate construction; about the specific activities; and sometimes about the configuration of the end product itself. There is little past history on which to base network construction and time estimates.

PERT takes some of these uncertainties into specific account. It assumes that the activities and their network relationships have been well defined, but it allows for uncertainties in activity times. For each activity in the project network, not only is an estimate made of the *most probable time* required to complete the activity, but some measure of uncertainty is also noted in this estimate. The person most qualified to know—an engineer, foreman, or worker—is asked to give two other time estimates. One of these is a *pessimistic estimate*—a best guess of the maximum time that would be required to complete the activity if bad luck were encountered at every turn. The estimate does not include possible effects of earthquakes, floods, fires or other highly unusual catastrophes, but it does reflect the sort of design or construction problems inherent in the situation. The qualified person is also asked to give an *optimistic estimate:* If everything goes right, how long will the activity take at the minimum? In other words, what is the shortest conceivable time for the completion of the activity?

These time estimates are not always easy to prepare, but together they give useful information about the expected uncertainties of an activity. For standard, rather straightforward activities (technologically speaking), the three estimates should not vary much from each other. But the greater the uncertainty of an activity, the wider will be the range of the estimated completion times. And the most probable time is not always the best guess of the time one should *expect* the activity to take. If the most probable time estimate is closer to the optimistic than to the pessimistic time estimate and if these two extreme values have about the same likelihood of occurrence, then the *average* or *expected time*, over the long run, will be influenced more by the pessimistic time and will be higher than the most probable time. This notion is illustrated below.

Expected Times for Activities

PERT calculates the expected value of an activity duration as a weighted average of the three time estimates. Specifically, it makes the assumption that the optimistic and pessimistic activity times, t_o and t_p, are about equally likely to occur. It also assumes that the most probable activity time t_m, is four times more likely to occur than either of the other two.[1] So if we apply these weights to the three time estimates, we come up with a formula for the average, or expected, time, t_e, of an activity:

$$t_e = \frac{t_o + 4t_m + t_p}{6}$$

The *expected time*, as the name implies, is what we would expect the activity duration to be on the average if the activity were repeated a large number of times. In most PERT applications, to be sure, activities don't get repeated a large number of times; they usually occur just once. But t_e is still the best estimate we can make of the time required for a single occurrence of an activity.

To further illustrate these concepts, consider the following example: A design engineer is asked to make three time estimates for the activity Design Stator Tube. Based on past experience with similar activities, he decides that the most likely activity time is 8 days. It is possible, he thinks, that the activity might be done in as few as 5 days but if problems arise, it might take as long as 17 days. Implicit in his estimates—and perhaps explicit in his own mind—is a whole range of possible durations; he has assigned to each some likelihood of occurrence. Most probably his likelihood measure wasn't reduced to quantitative values but thought of only in a relative sense. This might be illustrated by means of a graph showing a distribution of possible durations, each represented by a bar whose height represents some relative measure of likelihood, as in Figure 4–1.

Thus, 8 days has the highest likelihood; that is, it is the most likely or most probable time. On either side of 8 days the likelihoods are decreasingly lower. A duration of less than 5 days or more than 17 days is too unlikely to consider.

What we have drawn is very close to what the statistician calls a *probability distribution*—that is, a distribution of probability values for all possible outcomes. All we would have to do is to assign quantitative values, or probabilities, to our likelihood measures. By common agreement

[1] For the quantitatively inclined, the weights are based on an approximation of a statistical frequency distribution known as Beta. The Beta distribution was chosen, in turn, as a reasonable approximation of the distribution of activity times for reasons that seemed justifiable to the originators of PERT. The Beta distribution is unimodal (has a single peak value), has finite and non-negative end points, and is not necessarily symmetrical—all of which seem desirable properties for the distribution of activity times. (The normal distribution—more widely used and commonly known—fails to satisfy the last two criteria mentioned.) Note that the choice of a Beta distribution was not based on empirical data. Since most activities in development projects occur just once, frequency distributions of such activity times cannot be developed from past data.

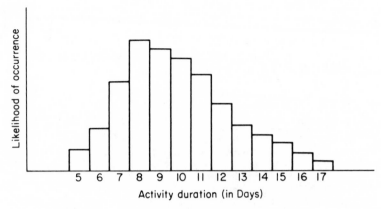

FIGURE 4-1. Distribution of Possible Durations for Activity "Design Stator Tube"

among statisticians, probability measures are always between 0 and 1, inclusive. If an event has a probability of 1, then it is certain to occur and if its probability is zero, then by definition, it can never occur. Any value between 1 and zero represents a possible occurrence. The closer the value is to 1, the more likely is the event.

In our example since the activity duration may assume any value between 5 and 17, inclusive, and since it must assume one (and only one) of these values, the probability measures assigned to each of these possible outcomes must total one. This is true of all probability distributions; that is, the sum of all possible, different outcomes must be one. Sometimes a probability distribution is represented by a curve rather than by a series of bars, indicating that a continuous range of outcomes is possible, not just certain specific values.[2] Since the sum of the probabilities of all outcomes must still be one, it can be shown that the area under a probability curve is also unity.

Going back to our example again, we can reason that the activity Design Stator Tube wouldn't necessarily take exactly 8 days, 9, 15, or any other integer number of days. It could take on any value between 5 and 17, including fractional values. Thus, our probability distribution in this case can best be represented conceptually by a curve, as shown in Figure 4–2.

The three estimates made by the engineer are identified on the curve. If we knew the exact shape of the probability curve, we could accurately calculate the average value of *t*, but since such precise curves are almost

---

[2]For example, if you flip a coin twice, there are just three specific outcomes possible: 0, 1, or 2 heads. Such a process repeated many times gives rise to a *discrete* distribution of outcomes. On the other hand, if the results of a process may take on any value over a range of possible outcomes, then the process yields a *continuous* distribution. Time, weight, distance, pressure, and temperature are all continuous measures.

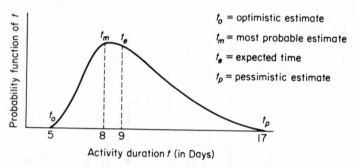

FIGURE 4-2. Continuous Probability Distribution

never available, we must use an approximation. The average, or *expected,* time as approximated by the PERT formula is:

$$t_e = \frac{t_o + 4t_m + t_p}{6} = \frac{5 + 4(8) + 17}{6} = 9 \text{ days.}$$

The fact that the expected time t_e is larger than t_m in this example is a reflection of the extreme position of the pessimistic time t_p. Its influence on the averaging process is to draw the average, or central, point of the distribution to the right of the peak value at t_m.

Variability of Activity Times

Not only is it useful to have a means of calculating the average, or expected, time required for an activity, but we need to know how reliable that estimate is. If the time required for an activity is highly variable—if the range of our estimates is very large—then we will be less confident of the average value we calculate than if the range were narrower. For example, if the three time estimates for the activity Design Stator Tube were 8, 9, and 10 days (for optimistic, most likely, and pessimistic times, respectively), then the average would still be 9 days, and we would be more confident of this figure than in the previous case where the estimates range from 5 to 17 days. Thus, a wide range of estimates represents greater uncertainty and hence less confidence in our ability to correctly anticipate the actual time that the activity will require. What we need, then, is a means of measuring the variability of an activity's time duration. If we know the variability, we can, in turn, measure the reliability of our expected time, as determined from the three time estimates.

One measure of variability of possible activity times is given by the standard deviation of their probability distribution. Standard deviation and variance are commonly used in statistics as measures of variability among numbers. The *variance* is simply the average squared difference of all numbers from their mean value, or average. For example, the average of 3, 4, and 8 is 5. The squared differences of these numbers from 5 are $(-2)^2$, $(-1)^2$, and $(3)^2$, or 4, 1, and 9. The average of 4, 1, and 9 is 4 2/3 (the variance). The *standard deviation* is the square root of the variance.

PERT simplifies the calculation of standard deviation (necessarily, as only three out of all possible values of the distribution are given). The standard deviation of t, shown as S_t, is estimated by the formula

$$S_t = \frac{t_p - t_o}{6}.$$

That is, S_t is one-sixth of the difference between the two extreme time estimates.[3] Thus, the greater the uncertainty in time estimates, the greater will be the difference in t_o and t_p and the more spread out will be the distribution curve. A high standard deviation, S_t, represents a high degree of uncertainty regarding activity time; there is a greater chance that the actual time required to complete the activity will differ significantly from the expected time, t_e.

In our previous example where the extreme time estimates for the activity Design Stator Tube were given as 5 and 17 days, the standard deviation would, therefore, be estimated as

$$S_t = \frac{t_p - t_o}{6} = \frac{17 - 5}{6} = 2 \text{ days.}$$

Since standard deviation is the square root of the variance of a distribution, then the variance of t is calculated for the above example as

$$V_t = \left(\frac{t_p - t_o}{6}\right)^2 = \left(\frac{17 - 5}{6}\right)^2 = 4.$$

The Expected Length of a Critical Path

The *expected length* of a sequence of independent activities is simply the sum of their separate expected lengths, which gives us a simple means of determining the expected length of an entire project. We calculate a t_e for every activity in the network of a project and determine the critical path

[3] This formula, too, is an approximation based on the observation that almost all of a unimodal distribution is contained within three standard deviations of the mean. (For a normal distribution this percentage is over 99.7, and no distribution has less than 89 per cent of its area within this range, according to Tchebycheff's inequality.) Hence statisticians frequently estimate the standard deviation of a unimodal distribution as roughly $\frac{1}{6}$ of the range of the distribution. This implies—in the case of PERT—that the optimistic and pessimistic estimates are not necessarily the absolute extreme points of the range of possible values but rather the points beyond which there is, at most, only a very small probability of occurrence.

in the manner described in Chapter 3. The expected length of the project T_e, then, is simply the length of the critical path, that is, the sum of the t_e's of all activities along the critical path.

Similarly, the *variance* of a sum of independent activity times is equal to the sum of their individual variances. Since T_e is the sum of t_e's along the critical path, then the variance of T_e equals the sum of all the variances of these activities. We will call this sum V_T; and, similarly, the standard deviation of the project length will be S_T.[4] Either the variance or the standard deviation gives us a measure of the uncertainty surrounding our estimated project time. The higher the S_T is, the more likely it is that the actual time required to complete the project will differ from the T_e. As with a single activity, though, the expected value T_e is the best time estimate we can make for the entire project—except in some circumstances that we shall note below.

As a simple example of how these PERT formulas are applied, we shall calculate the project length and variance for the network of activities illustrated in Figure 4–3.

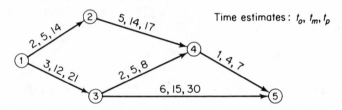

FIGURE 4-3. Example of PERT Calculations

Above each activity arrow are numbers representing the three time estimates t_o, t_m, and t_p, in that exact order. We have chosen these numbers for ease of computation rather than to illustrate actual PERT data. Using the PERT formulas for t_e and S_t, we arrive at the following results:

Activity	Expected Time	Standard Deviation	Variance
(1,2)	6	2	4
(1,3)	12	3	9
(2,4)	13	2	4
(3,4)	5	1	1
(4,5)	4	1	1
(3,5)	16	4	16

[4]If more than one critical path exists, the one with the largest variance is chosen to determine V_T and S_T.

The longest path of *expected* times, and hence the critical path, consists of activities 1,3 and 3,5, with a length $T_e = 12 + 16 = 28$. The variance of the critical path is then $V_T = 9 + 16 = 25$, which corresponds to a standard deviation $S_T = 5$. You may verify, if you wish, that the next longest path has a length of 23 with a standard deviation of 3 and that its activities all have total slack of 5.

To summarize thus far, PERT differs from CPM in its attempt to recognize uncertainty by using three time estimates. These are reduced to a single time estimate for purposes of calculating a critical path and for obtaining the kinds of network information we described earlier—early and late start times for each job, slack values, and so on. But the standard deviation for each activity and for the entire project gives the manager additional information about variations in job and project times that he can anticipate. He should, therefore, be better able to plan for and cope with such variations.

Probability of Completing a Project by a Given Date

How can S_T or V_T be translated into managerial terms? That is to say, what does a particular value for S_T tell the manager about the variability of a project's length? We have already indicated a qualitative answer to these questions: A large S_T is associated with a higher variability in the expected project length. But what is a *large* S_T? Can a more quantitative interpretation be given—one that will enable the manager to assess the meaning of a particular S_T for a particular project?

The answer is Yes, but an explanation to our answer requires the use of some elementary notions in statistics. The theory underlying these notions is not so simple, but an explanation can be given in a fairly straightforward fashion.

We mentioned earlier that the time required for an activity is uncertain: It may take on any value within a given range. Statisticians refer to such a measure as a random variable. Its value in a particular instance cannot be predicted with certainty, but its average, or expected, value (t_e) can be estimated on the basis of an assumption regarding the nature of its probability distribution and three points on this distribution—stated as the optimistic, most likely, and pessimistic times. As a weighted sum of random variables, t_e is also a random variable.

We calculated the average, or expected, project length, T_e, by adding the t_e's along the critical path. Since the t_e's are all random variables, then so is T_e. But the interesting (and fortunate, from a statistical standpoint) result is that T_e does not have the same distribution as the t_e's but follows approximately what is called a normal distribution, the familiar bell-shaped curve.[5] A normal distribution is symmetric with a single peak value, and it is described completely by its mean, or average, value and its standard deviation. That is, two normal curves with the same mean and standard deviation are always identical; there is no characteristic in which they can differ. Since we know much about the normal curve, we can infer a good deal of managerial information about a project's length if we know the expected length and standard deviation (T_e and S_T) of its distribution.

For example, 68 per cent of the area under a normal curve is within one standard deviation of the average of the distribution, as illustrated by the shaded region in Figure 4-4.

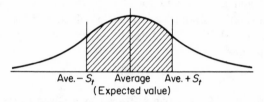

Ave. $- S_t$ Average   Ave. $+ S_t$
(Expected value)

FIGURE 4-4. Normal Probability Distribution

Since the area under a probability curve corresponds directly with probability measures, we can state the following conclusion: A random variable drawn from a normal distribution has a .68 probability of being within one standard deviation of the distribution average. In terms of project duration, the interpretation is analogous: There is a 68 per cent chance that the *actual* project duration will be within one standard deviation, S_T, of the estimated average length of the project, T_e. There is an even greater chance (better than 95 per cent) that the project duration will be within *two* standard deviations of the average, and it is almost certain (99.7 per cent) that the duration will not be more than three standard deviations away. All of this follows from basic statistical notions *if* the random variable "project length" is really normally distributed and *if* the estimated activity times are unbiased[6]—two rather large *if's*. But even if these assumptions aren't completely satisfied, the results of the analysis—if not precise—at least give useful guidelines to the manager. For example, if the above calculations applied to two proj-

[5]For the technically oriented, this result is inferred from the Central Limit Theorem, which implies that the sum of a large number of independent random variables will be approximately normally distributed, regardless of the distribution of the individual random variables.

[6]We use "unbiased" here in the statistical sense. An *unbiased* estimate is one which results from an estimating procedure which, on the average, yields the correct figure. Thus, if an engineer's estimates of activity times tend to be high (or low) on the average, the estimates are biased. If, on the other hand, some are high and some are low but their average is correct, then they are unbiased.

ects led to estimated probabilities for on-time completions of .20 and .95, respectively, a manager would certainly be more concerned about the former project than the latter and more likely to take corrective action on it, even if he knew that the actual figures might not be precisely correct.

Let's make the above procedure more concrete. Suppose that a manager has analyzed the project diagrammed in Figure 4–5 and has calculated the expected activity times and variances as recorded.

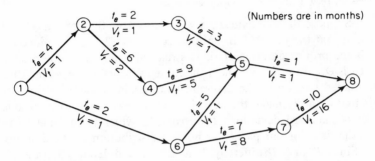

FIGURE 4-5. PERT Network with Expected Activity Times and Variances

You may verify that the critical path passes through nodes 1, 2, 4, 5, 8 and has an expected length, or T_e, of 20 months. The variance along this path, by PERT calculations, is the sum of the activity variances, or $V_T = 9$, which is equivalent to a standard deviation, S_T, of 3 months. If we assume that T_e is normally distributed, as illustrated in Figure 4–6, there is a probability of about .68 that the project length will be within one standard deviation of T_e—that is to say, between 17 and 23 months. This is because 68 per cent of the area under the probability distribution lies between the vertical lines at 17 and 23 months. Likewise, the probability is better than .95 that the project will not exceed the limits $20 \pm 2(3)$, or 14 months on the low side

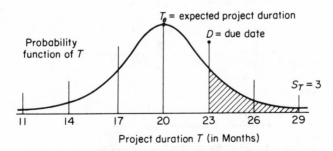

FIGURE 4-6. Distribution of Project Completion Times

and 26 months on the high side. One can be virtually certain (over .99 probability) that the project will take no less than 11 and no more than 29 months. Probabilities for any points in between those cited above can be calculated by referring to a standard normal table in almost any statistics book.

The same essential notions may be used to answer the question, What is the probability that the project will be completed by such-and-such a due date? Picture again the distribution of project completion times in Figure 4–6, based on our previous example.

Suppose the due date, D, is 23 months from the starting point. How likely is it that the project will be finished by then? Such an outcome will occur if the project duration, T, is less than or equal to 23, the probability of which is equal to the area under the curve to the left of 23, as indicated by the unshaded portion of the diagram. Once again, standard normal tables enable us to readily make this calculation. We have only to determine the number of standard deviations D is from T_e, which is equivalent to converting the data for our particular normal distribution to standard normal form.[7] Since T_e and D differ by 3 months, the difference represents one standard deviation (remember that $S_T = 3$). A formula for the calculation may aid the memory:

$$Z = \frac{D - T_e}{S_T}$$

Here Z is the number of standard deviations by which D exceeds T_e. Note that D might be less than T_e, in which case Z is negative. Now the probability measure originally sought may be obtained by referring to the following table, extracted from a standard normal table:

Z	Probability of meeting Due Date
3.0	.999
2.8	.997
2.6	.995
2.4	.992
2.2	.986
2.0	.977
1.8	.964
1.6	.945
1.4	.919
1.2	.885
1.0	.841

[7] A standard normal distribution has an average value of zero and a standard deviation equal to one.

.8	.788
.6	.726
.4	.655
.2	.579
0.0	.500
−.2	.421
−.4	.345
−.6	.274
−.8	.212
−1.0	.159
−1.2	.115
−1.4	.081
−1.6	.055
−1.8	.036
−2.0	.023
−2.2	.014
−2.4	.008
−2.6	.005
−2.8	.003
−3.0	.001

In our particular example, since $Z = 1$, then the probability of meeting the due date is about .84. To cite one more example, suppose that the due date is 17 months. How likely is it that the project will be completed by then? As before, calculate Z:

$$Z = \frac{D - T_e}{S_T} = \frac{17 - 20}{3} = -1.0$$

and the associated probability is close to .16. In other words, there is less than one chance in six that the project will be completed on time.

Effects of a Near-Critical Path[8]

We hinted above that T_e, obtained from adding the t_e's of critical path activities, might not always be the best estimate of project length. Here is why. It is possible that, under some combination of activity times and variances, a near-critical path may exist with a higher variance[9] than the "official" critical path. If bad luck is generally experienced with activities along this path and good luck with activities along the critical path, it is quite possible for the former to exceed the latter in length—that is, to become critical itself. Thus, where the possibility of uncertain activity times is admit-

[8]The next four sections may be skipped at first reading if desired.
[9]Actually, it doesn't have to be higher for the effect described to occur (it can even be lower); but the effect will occur more often in the circumstances described.

ted, the possibility of alternate critical paths is implied. We may be in error, then, in basing our estimate of T_e on the t_e's of a single critical path. Other paths may become critical and should influence our estimate of T_e.

Other Methods for Calculating Project Length and Variance

To illustrate, we shall again use our sample project of page 45, which is based on Figure 4–5. Recall that the critical path had an expected length, or T_e, of 20 months with an S_T of 3 months. By ordinary PERT methods, we would say that there was a .84 probability of finishing the project in 23 months (which represents one standard deviation above the mean). Actually, this is the probability that activities along the critical path, by themselves, will be completed in 23 months. It is usually assumed that noncritical paths can be ignored because they are shorter and not likely to affect the due date. But examine the sequence of activities along path 1–6–7–8. This path is 19 months long—only 1 less than the critical path. Furthermore, it has a standard deviation of 5 months, 2 *more* than that of the critical path. If we consider this 19-month sequence of activities by itself, the probability of its completion in 23 months is only .79, since Z $= \dfrac{23 - 19}{5} = .8.$

That is to say, the expected length of path 1–6–7–8 is 4 months less than the due date of 23 months, while the critical path's expected length is only 3 months shorter than the due date. Comparing just the expected lengths with the due date, we see that path 1–6–7–8 has more slack than the critical path. But because of the greater variability in time estimates of the former path (and hence a larger standard deviation), its chance of completion by the due date is less than that of the critical path. Furthermore, since *all* activities in a network have to be completed before the project is finished, the probability that *both* sequences of activities will be done in 23 months or less is .66, the product of their respective probabilities. (We have made some assumptions here—primarily that the activity durations are independent of each other. Also assumed is that the activities which connect with, but are not a part of, these two sequences do not affect the completion times of the sequences—which is very nearly true in this particular example.)

Thus the normal PERT procedure which bases the estimates of T_e and S_T on a single critical path can grossly overstate the probabilities of completing a project by a given date, especially if there are one or more parallel paths through the network which are nearly critical, and/or which have relatively large variances. The more there are of such paths, the more nearly critical they are, and the larger their variance, then the more serious will be the errors. A manager could think his chances of finishing a project on time were very good, when, in fact, they were very poor. On the other hand, if there are many interconnections between such parallel paths, or if the critical path is much longer than any other path, then the normal PERT calculations should lead to satisfactory results.[10]

Theoretically, it is possible to arrive at a mathematical expression for the expected length of a project by combining the statistical distributions for jobs in the project network.[11] But the expression becomes exceedingly complex and the calculations enormously tedious for anything but the smallest project and simplest assumed frequency distributions.

Simulation of a Network

A much more easily managed approach is simulation. By use of Monte Carlo sampling technique, activity times are randomly selected for each activity from some appropriate frequency distribution. The project length and critical path data are then calculated in the normal way, based on these times. This procedure is repeated perhaps several thousand times with a computer and a record is kept of the critical path data generated. Finally, an average project length and standard deviation are calculated on the basis of all this simulated data.[12] The resulting estimates should be more reliable than those produced by the normal procedure, since they take into account the effects of near-critical paths which may, in fact, become critical if activities along them take more than their normal times.[13]

Criticality Index

A new and useful measure of criticality can also be obtained from the simulated data. For each activity a record is kept of the proportion of simulation runs in which the activity is critical. For example, if activity *a* is on a critical path 3,000 times out of 10,000 simulation runs, then we would say that *a* has a criticality index of .30 for the given project. The activity may not have appeared at all on the critical path calculated by normal procedures,

---

[10]For an interesting analysis of errors that may result from the PERT assumptions, see K. R. MacCrimmon and C. A. Ryavec, "An Analytical Study of the PERT Assumptions," *Opns. Res.*, **12**, No. 1 (Jan. Feb. 1964), 16–37.

[11]See A. Charnes, W. W. Cooper, and G. L. Thompson, "Critical Path Analysis Via Chance Constrained and Stochastic Programming," *Opns. Res.*, **12**, No. 3 (May-June, 1964), 460–470.

[12]For a more detailed explanation of the methods, see R. M. Van Slyke, "Monte Carlo Methods and the PERT Problem," *Opns. Res.*, **11**, No. 5 (Sept. Oct. 1963), 839–860.

[13]The extent of PERT's tendency to yield overly optimistic estimates is examined by A. R. Klingel, Jr., in "Bias in PERT Project Completion Time Calculations for a Real Network," *Mgt. Science*, **13**, No. 4 (Dec. 1966), B-194 to B-201.

but the simulation tells us that the activity has about a 30 per cent chance of being critical, if the data upon which the calculations were made are accurate. Activities with the highest criticality index would be subject to the most managerial scrutiny, since they would have the highest probability of delaying the project. But a moderately high index would also call attention to near-critical activities; there would be less chance of their being ignored than in a case where a single critical path is identified and activities are either critical or not. Additionally, a probability distribution of slack values for each activity could be calculated. Rather than a single slack value, a range of slack values with associated probabilities would be identified with each activity.

Thus the simulation procedure helps to extend the notion of uncertainty to the critical path itself. No single path is identified as critical, but the probability of each activity's being on a critical path is estimated. If the concept of probability is understood by the project manager, the information provided by a simulation calculation should be much more useful than that derived from the conventional PERT calculations.

PERT's Event Orientation

Some writers have emphasized another difference between PERT and CPM: while CPM is activity-oriented, PERT is often event-oriented. Essentially, this means that in activity-oriented networks, the arrows representing activities or jobs are labeled with some description of the activity; while in event-oriented networks, the events are the objects of interest and are appropriately described. An activity represents a segment of work to be accomplished over a period of time, but an *event* is a point in time—a milestone representing the beginning or the completion of some activity or group of activities. Thus the activity Design Propulsion System might appear in a PERT network with an initial node labeled "Begin design of propulsion system" (or perhaps just "Begin systems design" if the design of other components also commences at that point). The final node for the activity might read "Design of propulsion system completed," or "Begin test of propulsion system" if the successor activity involves the work of testing the system. The emphasis on events has its roots in the *milestone method* of management, in which program progress is monitored in terms of success or failure in reaching certain important milestones at scheduled points in time.

Nothing in the network itself is affected by event-orientation. The same arrows and nodes with the same interconnections will result from networking a project whether the approach is activity- or event-oriented. In fact, both events and activities can be labeled if desired. The tendency seems to be towards activity labeling, however, as it is the activities with which engineers and managers are most directly concerned. Engineers design *activities*, not *events*. And when projects fall behind schedule, it is the critical *activities* which receive managerial attention.

Network *calculations* can also be activity-oriented or event-oriented. In the former case, time calculations center on activities as illustrated in the network of Figure 4–7.

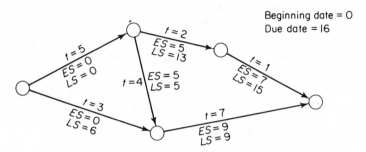

FIGURE 4-7. Activity-Oriented Network Calculations

Calculations follow the procedures outlined in Chapter 3. Early and late start times are recorded for each activity; finish times can readily be obtained by adding the appropriate activity durations. Event times are inferred from activity times: An event's early occurrence time, ET, is the latest EF of any activity preceding the event, while its late occurrence time, LT, is the earliest LS of any following activity.

Event-oriented calculations for the same network would have the results[14] illustrated in Figure 4–8. Since events consume no time, we don't

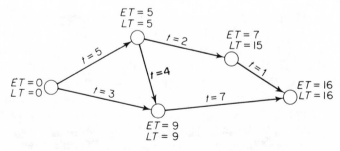

FIGURE 4-8. Event-Oriented Network Calculations

[14]Don't confuse this event-oriented arrow diagram with the AON diagram described in Chapter 2. In the former, activities are still shown as arrows and events as nodes, but network calculations are based on node occurrence times rather than on activity start and finish times.

calculate start or finish times, but only occurrence times, which may be early or late. Activity times can be derived directly from event times: An activity's early start equals the *ET* of its initial node, and its late finish equals the *LT* of its final node. As before, early finish time is obtained by adding the activity's duration to its early start, and late start equals late finish minus duration. Total slack can be calculated either for an event (*LT* minus *ET*) or for an activity (*LS* minus *ES*). Note that an event's slack is equal to the minimum slack of all paths which pass through the event node.

The two methods of calculation are equivalent, of course, and lead to the same results. Event-oriented calculations have certain advantages for computer programming, however. An example of an event-oriented computer program written in FORTRAN is given in the Appendix to this chapter.

The PERT Assumptions

Many thoughtful observers have questioned the assumptions upon which the PERT model is based. Some criticisms are of a technical nature—for example, is the assumption of a Beta distribution for activity times appropriate? Or, given that it is appropriate, does the simplified calculation, on pages 38 and 41, of expected activity time and standard deviation lead to error? MacCrimmon and Ryavec[15], in a searching analysis of the PERT assumptions, concluded that in certain extreme cases the simple formulas could lead to errors as high as 33 per cent in the calculation of activity lengths. If the Beta distribution is inappropriate for describing the distribution of activity times (which is not unlikely), then the error could be compounded. Since these errors can be either positive or negative, however, some cancellation of errors is likely to occur when activities are combined in a network.

Another important assumption is that activities are independent—that the time required to complete one activity will have no bearing on the completion times of its successors or of any other activities in the network. Conceptually, this might seem like a reasonable assumption, since activities —by definition—are independent endeavors; but in practice there are often dependencies. If one activity takes longer than expected, especially if it is on the critical path, then management will likely do what it can to expedite successor activities. In this indirect way the time of one activity can influence the time of another. Availability of resources can also result in dependencies. Two parallel activities which require the same limited resource may take longer than expected if they happen to be scheduled at the same time. (The limited resource problem will be examined in greater detail in Chapter

[15]*Op. cit.*

7.) Technological relationships are another source of dependencies. Such dependencies are supposed to be indicated on the project network by interconnections of activities, but it isn't always feasible or desirable to show *all* of these relationships, especially if the activities are at a high level of aggregation, encompassing many smaller activities.

Because of these and other sources of dependencies, the estimated project length and variance—especially the latter—may be in error. The first source of dependencies mentioned above (the effect of a job on its successors) would probably *reduce* the actual project variance as compared to the calculated value; the other two causes of dependencies would likely cause *greater* variability in project duration. A manager who is aware of these effects and who is familiar with the characteristics of a particular project might be able to anticipate—at least in some qualitative way—the net effects of these influences on the project duration. But they remain a problem of the PERT assumptions.

Other criticisms of the PERT model have come from *practitioners*—those who have had experience in applying it to "real world problems." However, we shall save for Chapter 8 our discussion of the difficulties which sometimes arise in applications of the PERT model.

Appendix: *A Critical Path Computer Program Written in FORTRAN IV*

The following program was written primarily to illustrate simple event-oriented critical path calculations. No attempt was made to include the more elaborate features of network programming or to allocate memory space efficiently. It is assumed that the data deck of project activities is in technological order (a subroutine could accomplish this if it is not) and that project data are punched in the following manner:

Card 1
    Field 1 (5 columns) Project Starting Date S
    Field 2 (5 columns) Project Due Date   D
    Field 3 (5 columns) Number of Activities
                  in Project   N

Cards 2 through $N+1$ (one card for each activity)
    Field 1 (5 columns) Activity Initial Node
                  Number   I(n)
    Field 2 (5 columns) Activity Final Node
                  Number   J(n)
    Field 3 (5 columns) Activity Duration   T(n)

Subscripted variables may be dimensioned according to the capacity of the computer and the size of the project expected. (A 32K machine should permit dimensions of about 2,500 words per subscripted variable, allowing projects of up to 2,500 activities to be handled). If activity durations are all whole numbers (as assumed in the program below), then all variables should be specified as integers. Otherwise, all but I and J should be declared real variables.

Variable names follow the mnemonic designations of the text (ES, LF, TS, and so on). I(n) and J(n) represent the i and j node numbers, respectively, of activity n, while T(n) is its duration time. All subscripts refer to activity numbers (ordered from 1 to N as they appear in the data deck) except for variables ET(k) and LT(k), for which the subscripts represent node numbers.

No output statements are included in the program. The interested reader may supply these, with output format as desired. The READ statements may have to be modified, depending on the particular compiler used.

```
      DIMENSION I(2500), J(2500), LS(2500), LF(2500)
      INTEGER T(2500), ES(2500), EF(2500), TS(2500), FS(2500), ET(2000),
     XLT(2000), S, D, TMIN
C     READ PROJECT START DATE, DUE DATE, AND NUMBER
      XOF ACTIVITIES
      READ 1, S, D, N
1     FORMAT (3I5)
C     READ ACTIVITY DATA—I NODE, J NODE, AND DURATION
      DO 2 K = 1, N
2     READ 3, I(K), J(K), T(K)
3     FORMAT (3I5)
C     INITIALIZE NODE OCCURRENCE TIMES
      DO 4 K = 1, 2000
      ET(K) = S
4     LT(K) = D
C     INITIALIZE TMIN, THE MINIMUM PROJECT DURATION
      TMIN = 0
C     FORWARD PASS—CALCULATE ES, EF FOR EACH ACTIVITY,
      XET FOR EACH NODE
      DO 5 K = 1, N
      INODE = I(K)
      JNODE = J(K)
      ES(K) = ET(INODE)
      EF(K) = ES(K) + T(K)
      IF (EF(K) − ET(JNODE)) 6, 6, 7
7     ET(JNODE) = EF(K)
6     IF (EF(K) − TMIN) 5, 5, 8
```

```
8   TMIN = EF(K)
5   CONTINUE
C   BACKWARD PASS—CALCULATE LF, LS, TS FOR EACH
    XACTIVITY, LT FOR EACH NODE
    DO 9 K = 1, N
    L = N + 1 − K
    INODE = I(L)
    JNODE = J(L)
    LF(L) = LT(JNODE)
    LS(L) = LF(L) − T(L)
    IF (LS(L) − LT(INODE)) 10, 11, 11
10  LT(INODE) = LS(L)
11  TS(L) = LS(L) − ES(L)
9   CONTINUE
C   CALCULATE FREE SLACK = ACTIVITY TOTAL SLACK
    XMINUS J NODE TOTAL SLACK
    DO 12 K = 1, N
    JNODE = J(K)
12  FS(K) = TS(K) − LT(JNODE) + ET(JNODE)
C   PRINT OUT RESULTS
    END
```

The above program bases the backward pass calculations on D, the due date. A minor change in the program could be effected if it were desired to base such calculations on TMIN, the minimum project length. Use of the PERT three time estimates could also be incorporated with little difficulty.

5

The CPM model

The Critical Path Method was originally developed to solve schedul-ing problems in an industrial setting. For this reason, probably, it was less concerned with the uncertainty problems that PERT attempted to cope with and more concerned with costs of project scheduling and how to minimize them. Thus, unlike PERT, CPM does not make use of probabilistic job times; it is a "deterministic" rather than a "probabilistic" model. It does, however, allow for variations in job times, not as a result of random factors (bad luck or good luck) but as the planned and expected outcome of resource assign-ments.

Most jobs, CPM argues, can be reduced in duration if extra resources (men, machines, money, and so on) are assigned to them. The cost for getting the job done may increase, but if other advantages outweigh this added cost, the job should be expedited, or *crashed*. On the other hand, if there is no reason to shorten a particular job—if it has a generous amount of slack—then the job should be done at its *normal* or most efficient pace, with a lesser assignment of resources. Thus, there is no need to crash all jobs to get a project done faster; only the critical jobs need be expedited. Which jobs to expedite and by how much are the problems CPM attempts to solve.

Schedule-Related Project Costs

The cost of a project is not due solely to the direct costs associated with individual activities, or jobs, in the project. Normally, there are indirect expenses as well—overhead items such as managerial services, indirect supplies, equipment rentals, allocation of fixed expenses, and so forth. Many of these are directly affected by the length of the project: The longer the time required for its completion, the higher will be these expenses. In addition, if the project management is under contract to a government agency or some other customer to complete the program by a given due date, often the contract will specify penalties for delay beyond this date. It was reported that Lockheed's contract for the C-5A contained a $12,000 per day late penalty clause, and that General Dynamics was rewarded $800,000 for flying the F-111 ten days ahead of schedule.[1]

Hence project schedules can influence two kinds of costs—direct costs associated with individual activities (which increase if the activities are expedited) and indirect costs associated with the project (which decrease if the project is shortened). Figure 5–1 illustrates these notions.

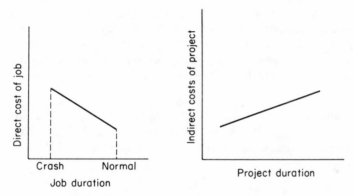

FIGURE 5-1. Costs Associated with a Project

As originally developed, the CPM model made the simplifying assumption that the time-cost trade-off for an individual activity is linear; that is, the relationship can be represented by a straight line on a graph plotting job duration versus cost. The steeper the slope of this line, the higher the cost of expediting the activity. A horizontal line, then, indicates that crashing the job would result in no decreased efficiency and, therefore, no added cost. One would normally expect the line to slope down to the right, indicating that costs go up as duration is reduced. If a job cannot be shortened regardless of the extra resources applied to it, then the line would be vertical. All three possibilities would likely be represented on a job's time-cost trade-off graph, such as Figure 5–2. Over a certain range, some decrease in time can be obtained by the application of extra resources (represented by the portion of

[1] *Aviation Week*, February 21, 1966.

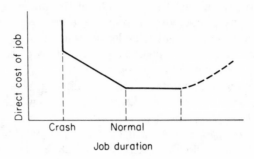

FIGURE 5-2. Time-Cost Trade-off Relationship for a Typical Job

the figure between "crash" and "normal"). There is probably a minimum duration, however, which cannot be further reduced no matter what the expenditure of resources (vertical portion of line). Similarly, slowing the job will decrease costs only up to a certain point; beyond this point no additional savings are obtained (horizontal portion of line). In fact, costs may take an upward turn if the job is excessively stretched out.

In reality, a curved line may better represent actual costs than a straight line or a piecewise linear line, as in Figure 5–2. Modifications of the original CPM model have made it possible to solve problems with other than linear cost-time relationships, but our discussion here will be confined to the simplest case.[2]

The Lowest-Cost Schedule

From an intuitive viewpoint, it seems likely that there is some optimum project length—a happy medium between one with excessive direct costs for shortening jobs and one with excessive indirect costs for lengthening the project. The CPM model verifies this notion mathematically, and it specifies a method for finding this *optimum point*—the point representing the least-cost schedule. The mathematics of the method are quite sophisticated,[3] but the general procedure can be easily explained.

To begin with, a preliminary schedule is generated in which all jobs are assigned at their early start times and with normal resources. This is the maximum length schedule; it can be reduced only by expediting one

[2]See the Appendix at the end of this chapter for an analysis of other possible cases.

[3]An outline of a linear programming formulation of CPM is contained in this chapter's Appendix. For an original source, see J. Kelley, "Critical–Path Planning and Scheduling: Mathematical Basis," *Opns. Res.*, **9**, No. 3 (May-June, 1961), 296–320.

or more of the jobs at added cost. If this added cost is less than the savings in indirect costs which result from shortening the project, then a less expensive schedule can be found. Improvements are made in stepwise fashion. New schedules continue to be generated as long as jobs can be crashed with a net reduction in total costs. The central problem, then, is to determine which jobs to expedite and how far to carry the schedule shortening procedure.

At each step of the process, only jobs along the critical path are considered for crashing. (We noted earlier that critical jobs are the only ones which affect project length; it can be reduced only by shortening one or more critical jobs.) The cost-time slope of each critical job is examined, and the job with the least slope is determined. This is the job that can be shortened with the least expense of added resources. If the cost of shortening the job one period is less than the resultant savings from shortening the schedule one period, then the job is expedited—up to the point where no further shortening of the schedule is possible (either because the job duration cannot be reduced further or because some other job has become critical along a parallel path). Then the remaining critical jobs are examined, and the one with the flattest cost-time line is selected. If there are parallel critical paths, then one job in each of them must be chosen for crashing. The process is repeated until no further shortening of critical jobs is possible or until the costs of such shortening would exceed the savings that result from reducing the project length.

Step-by-Step Example

A simple example should help to clarify these basic notions. Suppose we have a project consisting of four activities, connected as in the graph of Figure 5-3. Directly beneath each arrow (activity) is a pair of numbers. The first represents the normal time for the activity—the number of days required to complete the activity at its most efficient pace. The second number

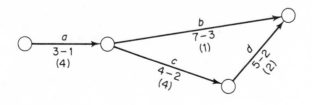

Key: Activity name

Normal time — Crash time in days
(Cost of crashing, $/day)

FIGURE 5-3. Example Network

represents the minimum time—the crash duration, which results from the application of additional resources. We assume that in-between points are possible, too. Noted in parentheses below the duration times is the cost per day of crashing—that is, the dollars of additional expense required to reduce the activity's duration by one day. For example, activity *a* normally requires 3 days. For 4 dollars added to its base cost, its duration can be reduced to 2 days, and for another 4 dollars it can be reduced to 1 day, the minimum possible time to complete the activity. Since every activity must be performed to complete the project, the *base cost* of every activity must be paid. These costs may be regarded as fixed, or "sunk," costs of the project. For decision-making purposes, the relevant activity costs are those associated with crashing—that is, the incremental expenses for reducing activity completion times.

Figure 5–4 shows the cost-time trade-off lines for each of the activi-

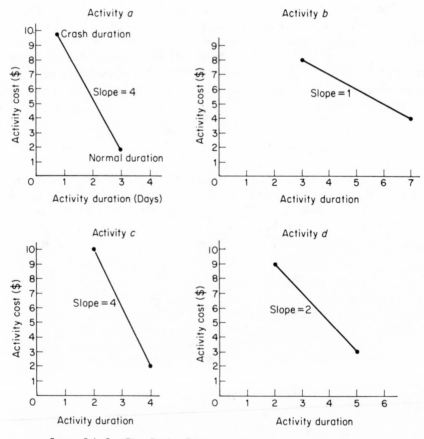

FIGURE 5-4. Cost-Time Trade-off Lines for Activities in Example Network

ties in our example. The slopes of these lines indicate the relative costs of crashing the activities: The steeper the slope, the more expensive it is to expedite an activity's completion. For example, activity c has a slope of 4;[4] it requires 4 dollars to shorten c by one day. By contrast, activity b has a flatter cost-time line, with a slope of 1. Thus, each day's reduction in activity duration costs just 1 dollar.

Suppose that time-related overhead expenses for this simple project are $4.50 per day. What is the least-cost schedule for completing the project? How much should each of the activities be accelerated, if at all?

To find the optimum schedule, we start with all activities at normal pace. The critical path then is *a-c-d*, and it is 12 days long, as shown in the schedule graph[5] of Figure 5-5.

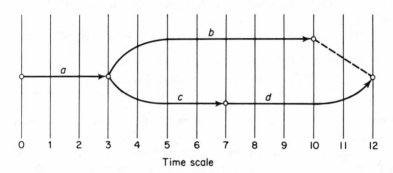

0 1 2 3 4 5 6 7 8 9 10 11 12

Time scale

FIGURE 5-5. Schedule Graph for Example Network

If we ignore the base costs of the activities, the cost of this schedule is $54:

$$\text{Cost} = \text{Cost of crashing} + \text{Overhead costs}$$
$$= 0 \qquad\qquad + (12 \text{ days}) (\$4.50/\text{day})$$
$$= \$54$$

To shorten the schedule would require crashing one or more activities on the critical path. Since d has the flattest slope of all critical jobs (see Figure 5-4), it can be shortened least expensively. We note also that b has 2 days of slack represented by the broken line. This means that d can be

---

[4]Mathematically, the slope of the cost-time line measures the increase in cost per unit *increase* in time. Thus, all of the lines shown in Figure 5-4 have negative slope. To simplify our exposition, however, we will ignore the minus signs and speak of the absolute values of the slopes.

[5]A *schedule graph* is a network drawn on a time scale, in which the horizontal length of arrows represents their duration and their placement on the scale reflects their scheduled start and stop times. Broken lines indicate precedence relations and the existence of slack.

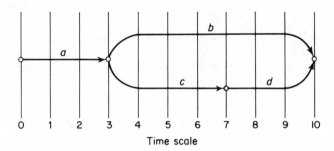

FIGURE 5-6. Ten-Day Schedule

shortened 2 days before *b* becomes critical. With this change in *d*, the schedule graph appears as in Figure 5–6.

The schedule is now ten days long and its cost is $49:

$$\text{Cost} = \text{Cost of crashing } d + \text{Overhead costs}$$
$$= (2 \text{ days}) (\$2/\text{day}) + (10 \text{ days}) (\$4.50/\text{day})$$
$$= \$49.$$

Although the cost of crashing increases $4, the overhead costs decrease $9, for a net improvement of $5.

Now we have two critical paths, *a-b* and *a-c-d*, and the schedule can be shortened only by reducing the length of both of them. Since *a* is common to both, a reduction in *a*'s length would accomplish our purpose. Or we could shorten the schedule by crashing one activity on each of the critical paths segments that are parallel to each other. There are two possibilities here: crashing *b* and *c*, or *b* and *d*. When two or more activities must be shortened jointly, their respective cost-time slopes must be added to obtain the cost of crashing. Thus our choices are as follows:

Crash Activity	Total Cost of Crashing $/day
a	4
b and *c*	$1 + 4 = 5$
b and *d*	$1 + 2 = 3$

Obviously, the last alternative is the most attractive, but note that *d* can be shortened only one more day before it reaches its minimum length of 2 days. (Remember that the second number for each activity in Figure 5–3 gives the minimum time required for the job.) Crashing *b* and *d* one day each results in the nine-day schedule of Figure 5–7.

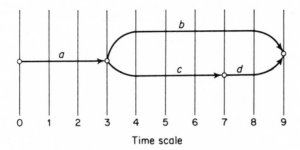

Time scale

FIGURE 5-7. Nine-Day Schedule

Schedule costs are now $47.50:

Cost = Cost of crashing b and d + Overhead costs

= [(1 day) ($1/day) + (3 days) ($2/day)] + (9 days)($4.50/day)

= $47.50

Of the remaining alternatives for reduction in project length, crashing a ($4/day) is less expensive than crashing b and c ($5/day). Activity a can be shortened from 3 to 1 days, and the schedule resulting from this change appears in Figure 5–8.

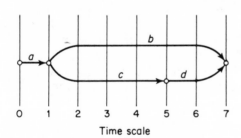

Time scale

FIGURE 5-8. Seven-Day Schedule

This seven-day schedule is costed as follows:

Cost = Cost of crashing a, b, and d + Overhead costs

= [(2 days) ($4/day) + (1 day) ($1/day) + (3 days) ($2/day)]

+ (7 days) ($4.50/day)

= $46.50

Now there is only one alternative for further reduction in schedule length: shortening b and c. Activity b has already been shortened by 1 day, but it can be reduced another 3 days. However, c can be shortened only 2 days. Even though the cost of crashing b and c exceeds the saving in over-

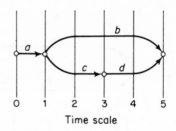

FIGURE 5-9. Five-Day Schedule

head, we perform this last change, which leads to the schedule graph in Figure 5–9.

This is the minimum length schedule. Even if b were further shortened, the project would still be five days long. The cost of the above schedule is:

$$
\begin{aligned}
\text{Cost} &= \text{Cost of crashing } a, b, c, \text{ and } d + \text{Overhead costs} \\
&= [(2 \text{ days}) (\$4/\text{day}) + (3 \text{ days}) (\$1/\text{day}) + (2 \text{ days}) (\$4/\text{day}) \\
&\quad + (3 \text{ days}) (\$2/\text{day})] + (5 \text{ days}) (\$4.50/\text{day}) \\
&= \$47.50,
\end{aligned}
$$

which, as anticipated, exceeds the cost of the previous schedule.

If we combine all of our results in a graph showing how project length affects total schedule costs, we obtain the curve in Figure 5–10.

With this information a manager can readily select the most appropriate schedule. Ordinarily, it will be at the low point on the curve, but frequently there are other factors, qualitative in nature, which the manager must also weigh. For example, perhaps the nine-day schedule entails fewer risks and greater safety for employees than the least-cost seven-day schedule.

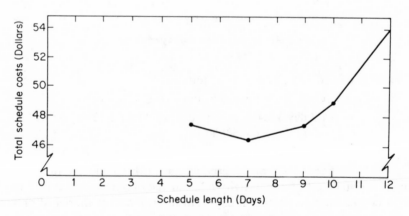

FIGURE 5-10. Project Cost-Time Curve

The difference in cost is slight and the increased safety may well be worth it in the manager's judgment. In any event, the project time-cost curve gives the manager explicit and useful information concerning the economic effects of project scheduling which, when combined with other relevant data and factors, should enable him to make better decisions.

What About "Stretching" Jobs?

Thus far we have implicitly assumed that a job is either done at what we have called its normal pace or else it is speeded up. But what about changing the pace in the other direction? Would it ever make sense for a manager to slow down a job, to stretch out its duration by a lesser application of resources?

The answer is, "It all depends." If slowing down a job will result in decreased efficiency and higher costs, then there is ordinarily little point to doing it. In most situations that we can think of, a project's utility is inversely related to its length. That is, a short overall project duration is preferred to a long one. This is usually true because it is desired to complete the project as early as possible and hence enjoy its benefits as soon as possible. If for some reason the project is to be completed by a fixed due date, the start date should be delayed as long as is prudently feasible. The latter follows from considerations of the time value of money and from the desire to minimize overhead costs that are related to the time duration of the project. The shorter the time that money is invested in a project before that money begins to reap benefits, the less costly is the financing of the project.

Thus it generally makes little sense to stretch out jobs if the effect is to increase both direct job costs and project overhead and financing costs. (There may be other factors involved, however, such as a limitation on resources that requires some jobs to be stretched out—a problem to be examined in Chapter 7. Also it may be desirable in certain circumstances to stretch a project beyond its optimal duration in order to maintain more stable employment levels, especially for companies engaged in multi-project activities where projects do not always dovetail precisely with each other.)

Is it possible, however, for direct activity costs to be reduced, at least up to some point, by a reduction in pace? If so, then how do we determine the optimum cost schedule by CPM?

According to most literature on CPM, this problem would not arise because the normal job time is defined to be the most efficient time also. An extended cost-time trade-off curve would then appear as in Figure 5-11 (a). But it is conceivable that normal time might be defined on some other basis than cost. The normal driving time between two cities might be one hour if a normal highway speed of sixty-five miles per hour is maintained,

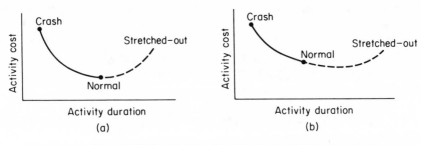

FIGURE 5-11. Two Activity Cost-Time Trade-off Curves

but a stretched-out travel time of ninety minutes would probably increase the mileage per gallon of gasoline and hence reduce costs. Thus if by normal we mean "what is ordinarily done, the usual or customary procedure," it is conceivable that the cost-time relationship might look like Figure 5-11 (b).

The CPM procedure described above may still be used, however, if we substitute the term "lowest cost time" or "most efficient time" for "normal time." This is really what the originators of CPM had in mind, but the meaning of terms differs from person to person, and it is advisable to clarify the point. Regardless of the terminology used, CPM ignores the portion of the cost-time curve (if it exists) to the right of the lowest point, a rule which can be logically defended in the absence of unusual circumstances such as those suggested above.

The Problem of Large Projects

The technique we have just illustrated may be described as an exhaustive search procedure because in the technique we looked at every possible alternative action at each step of the solution.

For simple projects not much larger than the one above, the optimum schedule may easily be found by such a manual search technique or by ones similar to it. As projects become larger, however, and as the number of jobs and paths through the network increases, the procedure becomes more and more difficult to follow because of the rapidly expanding number of alternatives to be evaluated at each step. Consider, for example, the twenty-four-job project illustrated in Figure 5-12.

There are twenty paths through the network. Can you identify them all? If all activities were critical (as might result from shortening the schedule), then every path would have to be made shorter in order to reduce the project length. Somewhere between two and six jobs, depending upon those chosen, would have to be crashed in order for all paths to be shortened, and there

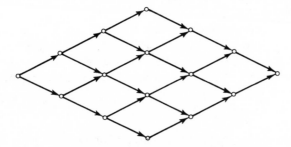

FIGURE 5-12. Twenty-Four-Job Project

are several *hundred* alternative ways of doing this. Clearly, it would require a great input of time and patience just to enumerate these alternatives by hand, and that is just one step in the repetitive procedure necessary to move to an optimum solution. Obviously, a project with several hundred or thousand activities (the typical size for real-life problems) would present an impossible task for a mere human who follows such a method. For most practical-sized problems, then, hand solutions are not feasible. More mathematically sophisticated techniques must be used, combined with the computational power of modern electronic computers.

Solution by Computers

In his original article referred to on page 58, Kelley described a linear programming procedure for finding optimal solutions for networks of jobs with linear cost-time trade-off curves. Other researchers have generalized his methods to handle nonlinear cost-time curves, and more efficient solution procedures based on network flow theory have been devised.[6] The Appendix to this chapter describes some of the linear programming formulations developed for cost optimization of critical path networks.

For the manager with a computer who wishes to apply CPM, more than sixty critical path computer programs are in existence, according to one survey.[7] Several of these programs have cost optimization features

---

[6] See E. B. Berman, "Resource Allocation in a PERT Network under Continuous Activity Time-Cost Functions," *Mgt. Science*, **10**, No. 4 (July, 1964), 734–745; D. Fulkerson, "A Network Flow Computation for Project Cost Curves," *Mgt. Science*, **7**, No. 2 (Jan. 1961), 167–178; W. L. Meyer and L. R. Shaffer, "Extensions of the Critical Path Method Through the Application of Integer Programming," Department of Civil Engineering, University of Illinois, July, 1963. Kelley, it should be noted, described a network flow algorithm in his 1961 article (*op. cit.*), along with a nonlinear extension of the method.

[7] See J. J. Moder and C. R. Phillips, *Project Management with CPM and PERT* (New York: Reinhold Publishing Corp., 1964), p. 254.

outlined in this chapter. One reportedly can solve networks with over 2,000 jobs and 1,000 nodes.

So far we have assumed that resources required for completing a job—whether at normal or at crash pace—are always available. The network calculations of both CPM and PERT are based upon this assumption. In the next chapter we shall examine problems that occur with network analysis when resources are limited.

A p p e n d i x: *Linear Programming Formulations of Network Problems*

Event-oriented network calculations are directly translatable into a linear programming formulation of the critical path algorithm. Let variable x_i represent the early occurrence time of node i, $i = 1, \ldots, m$ where $m =$ the number of nodes in the network. The objective is to minimize the difference between x_1 and x_m, where 1 is the first node and m is the last node in the network. (It is assumed that there is only one initial and one final node.) The constraints assure that the time difference between any two connected nodes, x_i and x_j, is at least as great as the duration, t_{ij}, of the connecting activity. Thus the general formulation is:

minimize $x_m - x_1$

subject to $x_j - x_i \geq t_{ij}$, all activities ij

 x_i unconstrained in sign, $i = 1, \ldots, m$

The usual solution procedure (simplex algorithm) will lead to a solution in which $x_1 = 0$, unless some other value is specified initially. Actually, any other x_i, including x_m, may be arbitrarily assigned an initial value without affecting the value of the minimizing function, since the latter measures only the difference between x_m and x_1 and the two vary directly with each other.

In the simplex solution, each independent variable x_i represents either the early or late occurrence time of its respective node (for nodes on a critical path the two times coincide). If it is desirable for *all* node variables to assume *early* occurrence values, then the following function will assure it:

minimize $x_m - x_1 + \sum_{i=2}^{m-1} x_i$

or, since x_1 is always $\leq x_m$,

minimize $\sum_{i=1}^{m} x_i.$

Similarly, if late occurrence times are desired, the function

minimize $m\, x_m - \sum_{i=1}^{m-1} x_i$

may be used. The m multiplier for x_m assures that the absolute value of the summation term in the function will never exceed the first term (since every $x_i \leq x_m$), which is necessary for a bounded solution. The effect is to push all x_i ($i < m$) to their upper bound without increasing x_m beyond its minimum value. It is assumed in all of the above, of course, that one x_i is constrained to a particular value, e.g. $x_i = 0$.

As an illustration of a basic linear programming formulation of critical path calculations, consider the simple project illustrated in Figure 5–13.

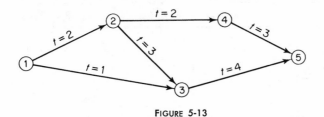

FIGURE 5-13

Since there are six activities, there will be six constraints, and the linear programming problem becomes:

minimize $x_5 - x_1$

subject to $x_2 - x_1 \geq 2$

$x_3 - x_1 \geq 1$

$x_3 - x_2 \geq 3$

$x_4 - x_2 \geq 2$

$x_5 - x_3 \geq 4$

$x_5 - x_4 \geq 3$

We can solve by the simplex method, or if we assign $x_1 = 0$, the solution may easily by obtained by inspection. Each x_i is simply assigned the smallest value permitted by the constraints, with the following results:

$x_1 = 0$

$x_2 = 2$

$x_3 = 5$

$x_4 = 4$

$x_5 = 9$

Actually, there are alternative solutions to the problem which will yield the same value of the function. Any node with slack may be increased by adding to it some portion of its slack, without changing the value of the function.

Nodal slack values may be obtained from node early and late occurrence times; the latter are calculated by assigning each x_i the *largest* value permitted by the constraints (but still maintaining the same x_m), or they may be inferred from activity slack values.

Activity slack is obtained directly from the simplex solution of the linear programming formulation. For example, the above problem has a final simplex tableau as shown.[8]

Basis Variables	Structural Variables					Slack Variables						Right-hand Side
	x_1	x_2	x_3	x_4	x_5	S_{12}	S_{13}	S_{23}	S_{24}	S_{35}	S_{45}	
x_2	-1	1				-1						2
x_3	-1		1			-1		-1				5
S_{13}						-1	1	-1				4
x_4	-1			1		-1			-1			4
S_{45}								-1	1	-1	1	2
x_5	-1				1	-1			-1		-1	9
Indicator Row $Z_j - C_j$	1	0	0	0	0	1	0	1	0	1	0	

Since each constraint is associated with an activity, slack variables necessary to convert inequality constraints to equalities are also activity-associated. S_{12}, for example, is the slack variable for the activity connecting nodes 1 and 2. Fortuitously, the terminology of linear programming or L.P. and CPM coincide: The slack variable (L.P.) takes on a value equal to the slack time (CPM) of an activity. From the tableau above, for example, $S_{13} = 4$, meaning that activity (1, 3) has 4 units of slack. Similarly, activity (4, 5) has slack of 2 units. Notice that slack variable S_{24} does not appear in the basis, indicating that $S_{24} = 0$ and that activity (2, 4) has no slack. By conventional CPM methodology, both (2, 4) and (4, 5) would have 2 units of total slack. At first blush, then, the analogy between conventional CPM calculations and the L.P. model does not seem complete. Slack in the L. P. model is relative to fixed values of node occurrence times (fixed by the solution procedure), and thus slack in a sequence of activities is all assigned to one of them only, depending upon nodal time assignments. If all such times are *early* occurrence times, then the slack will show up in the last activity of a sequence that leads into a path with less slack. In this case the slack is analogous to what we have called "free slack"— but in the formulation above,

---

[8] Artificial variables necessary to obtain an initial feasible solution have been omitted from the tableau. The tableau shown is not unique, as alternative solutions are available.

there is nothing to guarantee that all nodal times will be ET's. Notice in the indicator row of the final simplex tableau that there is a zero in the S_{24} column. Since S_{24} is nonbasic, this indicates that an alternate optimum solution exists. If S_{24} is brought into the solution, S_{45} goes out and the only other change is in x_4, which changes to 6. In effect, the alternate solution results in the assignment of node 4 at its late occurrence time, and a shift of slack from activity (4, 5) to activity (2, 4). If the alternate function described on page 68 were used, however, one could be assured that all nodes would be assigned at their ET's and the slack variables would represent activity free slack.

The dual of our original formulation has an interesting interpretation, also. The duality theorem of linear programming states that if a problem of the form (in matrix notation):

minimize $\quad\quad\quad \underset{(1 \times n)(n \times 1)}{cx}$

subject to $\quad\quad\quad \underset{(m \times n)(n \times 1)}{Ax} \geq \underset{(m \times 1)}{b}$

$\quad\quad\quad\quad\quad\quad \underset{(n \times 1)}{x} \geq \underset{(n \times 1)}{0}$

has a solution x^* which minimizes cx, then there is an analogous problem:

maximize $\quad\quad\quad \underset{(1 \times m)(m \times 1)}{wb}$

subject to $\quad\quad\quad \underset{(1 \times m)(m \times n)}{wA} \leq \underset{(1 \times n)}{c}$

$\quad\quad\quad\quad\quad\quad \underset{(1 \times m)}{w} \geq \underset{(1 \times m)}{0}$

which also has an optimum solution w^*, such that $cx^* = w^*b$. One problem is called the dual of the other, and it is arbitrary which is designated the primal and which the dual.

Note that if a primal has n variables and m constraints, then the dual has m variables and n constraints—just the reverse. There is a dual variable corresponding to each of the primal constraints and vice versa. It can be shown that if a primal constraint is stated as an equality (without slack variables), then the corresponding dual variable is unconstrained in sign. The opposite proposition also holds.

In the *solution* to a problem, if an inequality constraint in the primal is satisfied as an equality, then the corresponding dual variable must be nonnegative. But if the inequality constraint is satisfied as an inequality (that is, its slack variable is greater than zero), then the corresponding dual variable must be zero. Once again, the opposite, in an if-then sense, also holds; and for all propositions above, *primal* and *dual* may be interchanged.

The dual to our network problem follows directly from the duality theorem and the propositions above. Its general formulation is:

maximize $\sum\limits_{\text{all } ij} t_{ij}w_{ij}$

subject to $-\sum w_{1j} = -1$ all $1j$

$\sum w_{ik} - \sum w_{kj} = 0$ all $k \neq 1, m$

$\sum w_{im} = 1$ all im

$w_{ij} \geq 0$ all ij

As applied to the example network on page 69, the dual becomes:

maximize

$$2w_{12} + w_{13} + 3w_{23} + 2w_{24} + 4w_{35} + 3w_{45}$$

subject to

$-w_{12}$	$-w_{13}$					$= -1$
w_{12}		$-w_{23}$	$-w_{24}$			$= 0$
	w_{13}	$+w_{23}$		$-w_{35}$		$= 0$
			w_{24}		$-w_{45} =$	0
				w_{35}	$+w_{45} =$	1
$w_{12},$	$w_{13},$	$w_{23},$	$w_{24},$	$w_{35},$	$w_{45} \geq$	0

So stated, the problem may be given a *network flow* interpretation. The project network becomes a flow network. A hypothetical unit of flow (water, electricity, and so on) enters the initial node, travels through the network, and leaves the terminal node. Each w_{ij} represents flow through branch ij. If we follow the convention that flow into a node is positive and flow out of it is negative, then we can write a balancing equation for each node: *flow in = flow out*, or *flow in − flow out* = 0. The only known flows are those into the initial node and out of the final node so we place these unit constants on the right of the equal sign and all unknowns on the left, as above. Thus, there are as many equations as there are nodes. Each constraining equation above represents a flow balance on a particular node. For example, the second contraint says that flow into node 2 (w_{12}) minus the flow out of node 2 (w_{23} and w_{24}) equals zero.

The duration of an activity ij may be viewed as the cost (in time, money, or energy) of pumping a unit of flow from i to j in the network. Thus, the problem of finding the critical or longest path in a project network is equivalent to finding the highest cost route through the flow network. The function will be maximized when all flow is along that path which carries the highest costs (longest times). Because of the way the problem is structured —particularly the unit flow imposed on the network—all w_{ij}'s will be integer-valued and either 0 or 1. Thus, in the optimum solution the critical path is identified by activities having $w_{ij} = 1$. The function will then have a value equal to the length of the critical path. This will be the same as the optimal solution of the primal problem, which measures the difference between the initial and final node occurrence times. In the above problem w_{12}, w_{23}, and w_{35} are all one; the remaining w_{ij}'s are all zero, and the function has a value of 9.

A more complete development of the L.P. formulation of critical path scheduling is given by Charnes and Cooper in an article which first proposed the model.[9] As they state, linear programming is less efficient than the conventional CPM algorithm for obtaining a network schedule and critical path data, but it offers some advantages in that it provides access to the extensively developed L.P. literature. In particular, the features of duality and sensitivity analyses are available, with their useful managerial interpretations.

Cost Optimization—L.P. Models

The above L.P. model is time-oriented only; it does not consider the cost-time trade-off possibilities that were discussed earlier in this chapter. Further elaboration of the model is required to incorporate cost optimization in the solution procedure.

If we admit the possibility of expediting activities at some extra cost, then the activity time t_{ij} is no longer constant but becomes a variable in the L. P. model. The simplest cost-time relationship we can assume is a linear one as illustrated in Figure 5–14.

If, for convenience, we designate the absolute value of the slope by b_{ij}, then the equation for the line may be expressed as:

$$c_{ij} = a_{ij} - b_{ij} t_{ij}$$

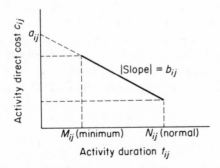

FIGURE 5-14. Linear Cost-Time Relationship: $c_{ij} = a_{ij} - b_{ij} t_{ij}$

[9] A. Charnes and W. W. Cooper, "A Network Interpretation and a Directed Subdual Algorithm for Critical Path Scheduling," *J. Indust. Eng.*, XIII, No. 4 (July-Aug., 1962), 213–219. The above adaptation of their material follows an opposite convention in signs so that event occurrence times are positive. Also, we have reversed the order of presentation and hence the designation of dual and primal.

where a_{ij} is the intercept of the projected line on the vertical axis, and t_{ij} is limited to values in the interval:

$$M_{ij} \leq t_{ij} \leq N_{ij}.$$

M_{ij} is the minimum duration achieved by crashing activity ij, and N_{ij} is its normal duration. Total costs for all activities would then be a function of the t_{ij}'s, as follows:

$$\text{Total direct costs} = \sum_{\text{all } ij} (a_{ij} - b_{ij} t_{ij})$$

Instead of minimizing project length, as before, the objective is to minimize project direct costs given a project length T. Since the a_{ij} are constant, direct costs can be minimized if we

maximize $\sum_{\text{all } ij} b_{ij} t_{ij}$

subject to $x_i + t_{ij} - x_j \leq 0$ all ij

$$t_{ij} \leq N_{ij}   \text{all } ij$$

$$t_{ij} \geq M_{ij}   \text{all } ij$$

$$x_m - x_1 \leq T$$

The first constraint, as in the earlier L.P. model, states that the difference in occurrence times of two connected nodes must be at least as great as the duration of the connecting activity. The next two constraints restrict each activity time t_{ij} to the interval between normal and crash times. Finally, the last constraint puts an upper limit on the project length. Note that T, an input parameter specifying this length, must be feasible. That is, it cannot be less than the length of the critical path with all activities at their minimum, or crash, times.

As a parameter, T may be varied to determine the effect of project length on direct activity costs. A plot of points thus obtained may be combined with indirect, or overhead, expenses corresponding to various project lengths to obtain the U-shaped total cost curve described earlier. Alternately, x_m could be incorporated in the objective function with a coefficient C representing time-related costs in dollars per time unit. The function would then become:

maximize $\sum_{\text{all } ij} b_{ij} t_{ij} - C x_m,$

and the last constraint above would be omitted, unless it was desired that the schedule length not exceed T. If the constraint is omitted, then one x_i must be fixed, e.g. $x_1 = 0$.

Note that, while the simple L.P. model on page 68 contained m variables and n constraints (where m = number of nodes and n = number of activities), the cost-optimization L.P. model contains $(m + n)$ variables and $(3n)$ constraints. Even a 100-job project—small by most standards—

would result in a large L.P. problem and require a considerable amount of computer time to solve. More efficient methods of solving the problem utilizing network flow theory are available.[10] Our purpose here, however, is to show as clearly as possible how CPM cost-optimization problems may be analyzed and formulated.

Nonlinear Cost-Time Trade-off Curves

Suppose that the cost-time relationship for an activity is not linear but curved, as shown in Figure 5–15.

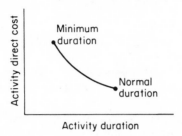

FIGURE 5-15. Continuous, Nonincreasing, Convex Cost-Time Curve

The curve implies that successive decreases in activity duration are increasingly expensive as that duration is reduced. This is intuitively plausible: For many activities the first 10 per cent reduction comes relatively easily, but the second 10 per cent is more difficult and therefore more expensive to achieve. Further cuts are even more costly.

The curve we have shown is continuous, convex, and nonincreasing. A relatively simple way to incorporate such a relationship in the L.P. model is to approximate the curve with linear sections. Any number of sections may be used, depending upon how close an approximation to the curve is desired, but for illustrative purposes suppose we approximate the above curve with two linear sections, as in Figure 5–16.

In effect we have replaced the original activity with two surrogate activities in sequence, the first having normal and crash times of P and M, respectively, with a cost-time slope of b_1. The second has normal and crash times of $N - P$ and 0, respectively, and a slope of b_2. Since $b_2 < b_1$, the CPM algorithm will always select activity 2 for crashing before activity 1. If both activities are scheduled at normal pace, their total time will be

[10] See D. Fulkerson, "A Network Flow Computation for Project Cost Curves," *Mgt. Science*, **7**, No. 2 (Jan., 1961), 167–178, and J. Kelley, "Critical-Path Planning and Scheduling: Mathematical Basis," *Opns. Res.*, **9**, No. 3 (May-June, 1961), 296–320.

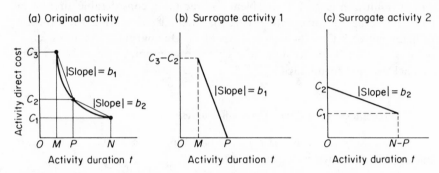

FIGURE 5-16. Piecewise Linear Approximation to Convex Cost-Time Curve

$P + (N - P) = N$ with a cost of c_1, the same as the original activity. If only activity 2 is crashed, the total duration will be $P + 0 = P$ with a cost of c_2. If both activities are crashed, the total time will be $M + 0 = M$ and the cost will be $(c_3 - c_2) + c_2 = c_3$, corresponding once again to the original activity.

The L.P. model will be essentially the same as before (page 74), except for the portions of it pertaining to activity ij:

maximize $\cdots b_1 t_{1ij} + b_2 t_{2ij} \cdots$

subject to $\vdots$

$$x_i + t_{1ij} + t_{2ij} - x_j \leq 0$$
$$M \leq t_{1ij} \leq P$$
$$0 \leq t_{2ij} \leq N - P$$
$$\vdots$$

(Note that b_1, b_2, M, P, and N, while not so subscripted here, still pertain to a particular activity ij.)

If the piecewise-linear approximation to an activity's cost-time curve contains k segments, then the activity is replaced by k surrogate activities in sequence and the solution procedure is entirely analogous to the above, as long as the cost-time curve is continuous, convex, and nonincreasing.

Nonconvex and Discontinuous Cost-Time Trade-off Curves

Integer programming must be resorted to if an activity's cost-time trade-off relationship is like any of those depicted in Figure 5–17. Curve (a) is continuous, nonincreasing, and—unlike the previous case analyzed—concave. The same method we used on the convex curve (Figure 5–16) could be applied to it, as illustrated in Figure 5–18; but since $b_1 < b_2$, the conventional solution procedure would pick surrogate activity 1 for crashing before

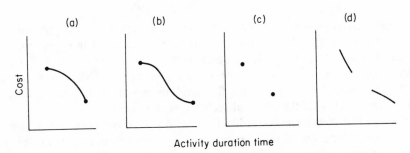

FIGURE 5-17. Other Possible Cost-Time Trade-off Relationships

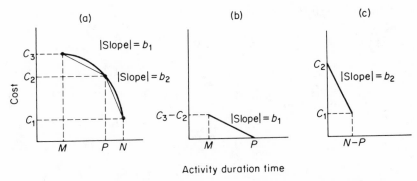

FIGURE 5-18. Piecewise Linear Approximation to Concave Cost-Time Curves

surrogate activity 2. In physical terms this is not meaningful. At normal pace the activity 1 requires N time units. The initial expediting is accomplished at the approximate rate of b_2 dollars per time unit of reduction. Only after the time is reduced to P units, can the lower rate of b_1 be realized. Activity 2's duration, t_{2ij}, must therefore be reduced to zero before any decrease in activity 1 is attempted.

One approach for assuring that line segments approximating a curve are brought into the solution in their proper order involves the use of an integer-valued variable, δ. To the constraints on page 76 are added the additional inequalities

$$\delta P \leq t_{1ij}$$
$$\delta(N - P) \geq t_{2ij}$$
$$\delta = \text{a non-negative integer.}$$

Taken together, these constraints restrict δ to the values of 0 and 1, which can more readily be seen if we solve the first two constraints in terms of δ. Combined they result in

$$t_{2ij}/(N - P) \le \delta \le t_{1ij}/P.$$

If the activity is scheduled at its normal rate, then $t_{2ij} = N - P$ and $t_{1ij} = P$, and consequently $\delta = 1$. If the duration is reduced, then t_{2ij} approaches zero, but as long as $t_{2ij} > 0$, then δ must remain equal to one and t_{1ij} equal to P. Only when $t_{2ij} = 0$ can $\delta = 0$ and t_{1ij} take on any value less than P. Thus segment 2 is brought into the solution procedure before segment 1, in accordance with the physical realities of the problem.

The method may readily be extended to more than two segments and to relationships that are neither convex nor concave, as in (b) of Figure 5–17. Suppose that an activity's cost-time curve may be approximated by r linear segments, as in Figure 5–19. In the general L.P. model, *each* activity ij contributes the following terms:

maximize $\quad \displaystyle\sum_{k=1}^{r} b_k t_k$

subject to $\quad d_o + \displaystyle\sum_{k=1}^{r} t_k + x_i - x_j \le 0$

$$0 \le t_k \le d_k - d_{k-1}, \qquad\qquad k = 1, \ldots, r$$

$$\frac{t_{k+1}}{d_{k+1} - d_k} \le \delta_k \le \frac{t_k}{d_k - d_{k-1}}, \qquad k = 1, \ldots, r - 1$$

$$\delta_k \ge 0 \qquad\qquad\qquad k = 1, \ldots, r - 1$$

$$x_i, x_j \ge 0$$

$$\vdots$$

The ij subscripts were omitted for simplicity of expression. In the complete formulation, all of the above terms would be repeated for each activity, and the following variables and constants would contain the subscript ij: b, d, t, r, and δ.

Activities are frequently encountered which can be expedited only

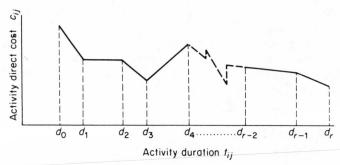

FIGURE 5-19. Piecewise Linear Approximation to General Cost-Time Curve

by changing the method of operation, resulting in a discontinuous cost-time trade-off curve. As a simple example, the activity "Mail package from Los Angeles to New York" may require three days and $10 if sent first class by rail, or one day and $16 if airmailed by jetliner. This would give rise to a relationship such as in Figure 5-17 (c). Even more frequently, resources can be increased only in discrete amounts; the result is a discontinuous curve, perhaps with multiple discrete points. Grading a roadbed for highway construction, for example, might be done with one, two, three, or four bulldozers; each possibility results in a distinct point on the cost-time trade-off curve. Where resources are not smoothly divisible, the assumption of a continuous trade-off curve may yield erroneous results.

Suppose that a discontinuous curve for activity ij consists of r discrete points with activity durations $d_1, d_2, \ldots, d_r$ and corresponding costs $c_1, c_2, \ldots, c_r$. Define a variable $\alpha_k, k = 1, \ldots, r$, such that $\alpha_k = 1$ when the duration is d_k, and zero otherwise. Then a linear program may be formulated as follows (we show only the terms involving ij):

minimize $\quad \cdots + \sum_{k=1}^{r} \alpha_k c_k + \cdots$

subject to $\quad\vdots$

$$x_i + \sum_{k=1}^{r} \alpha_k d_k - x_j \leq 0$$

$$\sum_{k=1}^{r} \alpha_k = 1$$

$$\alpha_k = \text{non-negative integers}$$

$\vdots$

This formulation for discrete cost-time relationships, combined with the formulation for continuous curves on page 78, may be applied to more complicated trade-off functions such as that illustrated in Figure 5-17 (d). Meyer and Shaffer develop in detail the procedures required.[11] The difficulty of such formulations, as mentioned above, is in their solution. Even a small project leads to a sizable L.P. model, especially if discontinuities are involved and the model must be augmented to assure integer solutions of certain variables. Meyer and Shaffer stated that a project with no more than fifty activities could be solved using computers and programs available in 1963, the time of their study.[12] Although larger and faster computers are available today, the L.P. approach is still limited to relatively small networks. Much more efficient

[11]See W. L. Meyer and L. R. Shaffer, "Extensions of the Critical Path Method Through the Application of Integer Programming," Department of Civil Engineering, University of Illinois, July, 1963.

[12]IBM 7090, using SHARE Library Code IP92 integer programming program. The main limitation was computer memory capacity.

network flow techniques may be used, however, if the cost-time trade-off curves are continuous, convex, and nonincreasing. Networks with thousands of activities may be solved even on moderate-sized computers. The interested reader is referred to Fulkerson or Kelley,[13] or to Moder and Phillips[14] for a concise exposition.

[13]D. Fulkerson, "A Network Flow Computation for Project Cost Curves," *Mgt. Science*, 7, No. 2 (Jan. 1961), 167–178; J. Kelley, "Critical-Path Planning and Scheduling: Mathematical Basis," *Opns. Res.*, 9, No. 3 (May-June, 1961), 296–320.

[14]J. J. Moder and C. R. Phillips, *Project Management with CPM and PERT* (New York: Reinhold Publishing Corp., 1964).

6

PERT/Cost: a network

cost accounting system

In their original developments, both PERT and CPM were essentially time-oriented. As planning tools they enabled managers to estimate the *time* required to complete a proposed project. As scheduling techniques they provided a means of establishing *time* schedules for project activities. And as control devices they allowed managers to check scheduled *times* against actual *times* for activity durations or event occurrences. While it is true that CPM included a cost-time trade-off feature, costs were to be considered only as a means of finding activity times. No provision was described in early CPM literature for compiling activity costs which resulted from the optimizing process in order to obtain total project costs, either for predictive or control purposes. Thus the output of the original CPM model was a list of optimal activity *times* (durations), generally with associated early and late start schedules, rather than a list of activity costs or a project cost summary.

Users (and critics) of CPM and PERT early commented on the need for an extension of these network techniques into the area of cost control. They argued that managers are concerned with activity costs as well as with elapsed activity times. Cost control is usually as important as time or schedule control—and frequently even more so. The incorporation of cost features in PERT and CPM seemed like a logical and desirable extension of these models, but several years elapsed after their introduction before network cost control systems were developed and made generally available.

A few individual users devised procedures of their own during the early years of network analysis, but the major impetus to cost control systems came with the publication in 1962 of a U. S. government manual, *DOD and NASA Guide, PERT Cost Systems Design*. Within a year the Department of Defense and the National Aeronautics and Space Administration required the user of PERT/Cost procedures on many military research and development contracts. Firms which bid in competition for such contracts—especially those involving large projects—had to demonstrate their capability and intention of using PERT/Cost as a management control technique. Progress reports and auditing procedures were to be tied to such a system.

While the government's sponsorship and endorsement of PERT/Cost undoubtedly accelerated its use and acceptance, such endorsement also had some negative effects. Many firms doing business with the government resented the strong pressure to install a completely new cost accounting system. Not only was it costly and difficult to do so, but they felt it was an unnecessary duplication of their existing systems. Perhaps some of the initial resistance to the PERT/Cost system was due to the government's somewhat forceful method of introducing it. Not only did the coercion cause resentment, but also there was an implied criticism of existing cost accounting systems which firms had developed over a period of years. And (though few firms would admit it publicly) there was the possibility that the PERT/Cost system would supply more information to the government about the firm's costs than the firms would like to give. Whatever the reasons, it is interesting to note that PERT/Cost or CPM/Cost systems were voluntarily adopted by many nondefense organizations with fewer complaints and a good deal more enthusiasm than was exhibited by those firms who were forced into adopting them.[1] Acceptance of the system, however, has grown over the years among both defense and nondefense industries. Managers have recognized the usefulness of information supplied to them by PERT/Cost accounting procedures.

Basic Concepts of Network Cost Systems

The basic concept of the PERT and CPM cost systems[2] is simple but importantly different from that of most cost accounting systems. In essence it is this: Costs are to be measured and controlled primarily on

---

[1] As further verification of the old saw, "You can lead a horse to water, but you can't make him drink," several firms doing business with the government set up PERT/Cost systems *in addition* to their regular cost accounting systems, using the former only to supply required documents and reports to the government and the latter for their own accounting and control purposes.

[2] The term "PERT/Cost" has acquired a somewhat generic status as a description of network cost accounting systems. We will use the term hereafter for convenience and economy of expression.

a project basis, rather than according to the functional organization of a firm. That is to say, individual activities or groups of activities form the micro cost centers for accounting (and therefore management control) purposes, rather than organizational units (divisions, departments, sections, and so forth). The rationale of the system is the entirely logical notion that responsibility for expenditures should coincide with responsibility for managing that which gives rise to the expenditures. Under a PERT or CPM management system, project managers and submanagers ordinarily are chosen for supervising individual activities or groups of activities. Since they are responsible for seeing that activities are completed on schedule, it is argued, they should also be responsible for controllable costs associated with the activities.

Cost overruns under a PERT/Cost system are more easily detected, and corrective action more readily taken. For example, under a departmental cost system, if expenditures were higher than expected in the engineering department, this might be due to any of a number of projects or activities upon which the engineering department was currently working. But if costs were measured and reported on an activity basis, an overrun could be immediately pinpointed to the particular activity responsible, and corrective measures could be initiated. This, basically, is the argument for a project-oriented cost accounting system.

These concepts are easier to describe, however, than to implement. In the first place, not all companies engaged in project work organize on a project basis; some feel that a functional organization is still superior. Others have attempted to combine features of both. Hughes Aircraft Company, for example, developed a "staff overlay" system in which project managers were assigned authority over certain segments of the line organization totally committed to their projects. Even with a project-oriented organization there are questions of how to organize certain functions, such as the legal department, on a project basis—or whether to attempt it at all. Many interests and conflicting views will be present in any firm. Even if organizational problems are resolved in a satisfactory manner, there will still be problems of cost allocations which are not easily solved—such as how to allocate overhead costs to various activities. Some of these problems will be discussed later in this chapter.

We should mention here, however, that a project-oriented cost accounting system does not necessarily replace existing systems based on organizational structure. A firm will probably plan budgets and report expenditures both on a project and on an organizational basis. If costs are identified with the proper degree of detail, cost summaries can readily be generated on either basis. Project-oriented cost control, however, generally requires an increased amount of detail in cost accounting records. Depending on how well the system is designed, it can either assist the manager with better information or deluge him with far too much of it. At least it has the potential, if used properly, of providing him with the kinds of cost information that should enable him to do a better job of planning and control than is possible under conventional cost systems.

Cost Accounting by Work Packages

As noted above, the basic idea of the PERT/Cost system is to measure and control costs in terms of the same entities of the project as are used for planning and scheduling purposes—that is, the activities. Actually, if a project has been broken down into activities small enough to be used for purposes of detailed planning and scheduling, many such activities would be too small to be used conveniently for cost control purposes. If so, several related activities may be grouped together into larger "work packages." These represent particular units of work for which responsibility can be clearly defined and which are still small enough to be manageable for planning and control purposes. The *DOD and NASA Guide* describes the organization of work packages in the following manner:[3]

> *End Item Subdivisions.* The development of the work breakdown structure begins at the highest level of the program with the identification of project end items (hardware, services, equipment, or facilities). The major end items are then divided into their component parts (e.g., systems, subsystems, components), and the component parts are further divided and subdivided into more detailed units. . . . The subdivision of the work breakdown structure continues to successively lower levels, reducing the dollar value and complexity of the units at each level, until it reaches the level where the end item subdivisions finally become manageable units for planning and control purposes. The end item subdivisions appearing at this last level in the work breakdown structure are then divided into major work packages (e.g., engineering, manu-facturing, testing). At this point, also, responsibility for the work packages will be assigned to corresponding operating units in the contractor's organization.
>
> The configuration and content of the work breakdown structure and the specific work packages to be identified will vary from project to project and will depend on several considerations: the size and complexity of the project, the structure of the organiza-tions concerned, and the manager's judgment concerning the way he wishes to assign responsibility for the work. These considerations will also determine the number of end item subdivisions that will

[3]Pp. 27 and 29.

be created on the work breakdown structure before the major work packages are identified and responsibility is assigned to operating units in a contractor's organization.

Further Functional or Organizational Subdivisions. An organization unit will usually identify smaller work packages within the major work packages assigned to it. This divison of work may take the form of more detailed functional (e.g., engineering) identification, such as systems engineering, electrical engineering, mechanical engineering, or it may take the form of a more detailed end item identification with engineering, such as instrumentation engineering, power cable engineering, missile section assembly engineering, and so forth. . . . The form chosen for more detailed identification will depend, again, on the structure of the performing organization and the manager's judgment as to the way he wishes to assign responsibility for the work. The *number* of these smaller subdivisions will naturally depend on the dollar value of the major work packages and the amount of detail needed by the manager to plan and control his work. Normally, the *lowest level* work packages will represent a value of no more than $100,000 in cost and no more than three months in elapsed time.

The work packages formed at the lowest level of breakdown, then, constitute the basic units in the PERT cost system by which actual costs are (1) collected and (2) compared with estimates for purposes of cost control.

The specific figures of $100,000 and three months duration are intended as guides rather than strict limits. The nature of a particular work package may logically lead to exceeding these figures in some instances. It should be remembered, also, that the *DOD and NASA Guide* was written primarily for the aerospace industry. Other industries or organizations might find different and more suitable methods of breaking down a project network for activity accounting. A construction contractor, for example, might select work packages on the basis of subcontracted jobs or upon the basis of the skills involved. In some cases a work package may be identical to a single activity on the project network, or it may embrace several activities in a subnetwork. The principle stated in the last paragraph quoted above is a generally useful guide to the selection of work packages for activity accounting.

Forecast of Project Costs

For planning and budgeting purposes, it is useful for a manager to know what the time pattern of expenditures will be for a project. If costs are estimated for each activity or work package,[4] then a projection of costs can easily be made, based upon an early start or a late start schedule or any other feasible schedule, for that matter. To do this, the assumption is usually made that expenditures for an activity are incurred at a constant rate over the duration of the activity. If this assumption is not valid for certain activities, they should be divided into a sequence of two or more subactivities, each of which has a relatively constant expenditure rate. Then the cost per period of an activity may be approximated by dividing its total cost by its duration in periods. A project cost schedule is then prepared by adding all activity costs, period by period, according to the activity time schedule.

As a simple example, consider again the project network in Figure 4–5, with activity costs added as shown in Figure 6-1.

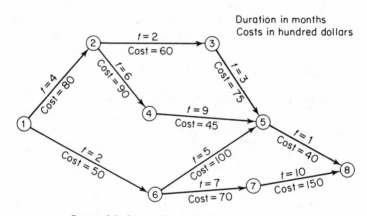

FIGURE 6-1. Project Network with Activity Costs

From the data shown on the network, Table 6–1 may be compiled following the methods discussed in Chapter 3. The only new data are the cost figures. A start time of 0 and a due date of 20 months are assumed.

Now a month-by-month summary of cost requirements is calculated for both early and late start schedules. In the first month, for example, activities (1, 2) and (1, 6) are active in the early start schedule, for a total cost of $20 + 25 = 45$ hundred dollars. In the fifth month, to illustrate further, activities (2, 3), (2, 4), (6, 5), and (6, 7) all occur, with joint costs of 75 hundred dollars.

A schedule graph, in which the network is plotted on a time scale and in which the horizontal length and placement of activity arrows indicate activity duration and schedule, facilitates cost calculation. Figure 6-2 shows

---

[4]For convenience, we will continue to use the term "activity" for either activity or work package.

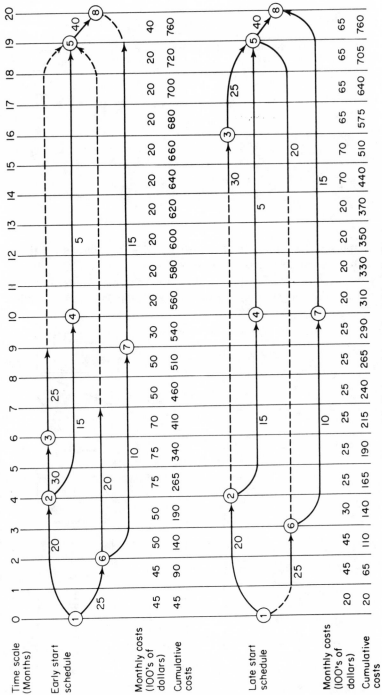

FIGURE 6-2. Early and Late Start Schedule Graphs

87

TABLE 6-1

Activity	Duration (months)	Early Start Time	Late Start Time	Total Cost (100 dollars)	Cost per Month (100 dollars)
(1,2)	4	0	0	80	20
(2,3)	2	4	14	60	30
(2,4)	6	4	4	90	15
(3,5)	3	6	16	75	25
(4,5)	9	10	10	45	5
(1,6)	2	0	1	50	25
(6,5)	5	2	14	100	20
(6,7)	7	2	3	70	10
(5,8)	1	19	19	40	40
(7,8)	10	9	10	150	15

schedule graphs of the project for both early and late activity start times. Monthly costs and cumulative costs are noted below each graph.

When plotted as in Figure 6–3, the cumulative cost figures illustrate more graphically the budget implications of the early and late start schedules.

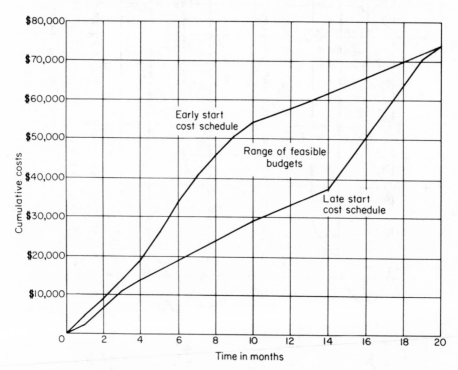

FIGURE 6-3. Cumulative Costs for Early and Late Starts

The area between the two curves represents a range of budgets which are feasible from a technological viewpoint. For budgetary or other reasons, it may be preferable to follow a relatively straight line of cumulative costs from start to finish. As long as this lies in the feasible region, it may be approximately achieved by juggling the scheduled starts of activities between their early and late start times.

Budget restrictions frequently limit the amount of expenditure in any one period, or certain critical resources—men, materials, machinery, and so on—may be available only in limited amounts. If budgetary or other resource constraints are such that even the late start cost schedule cannot be met, then the finish date must be delayed and the activities must be scheduled according to methods such as those to be discussed in Chapter 7. Once a schedule has been found which is feasible in terms of both technology and resource availabilities, however, a cost schedule may be calculated and plotted as above. A computer may be used to advantage for large projects, of course.

Analysis and Control of Project Costs

Basic to most cost control systems is a procedure for comparing actual costs with budgeted costs. The PERT/Cost system not only permits such a comparison but, because of its integration with project scheduling procedures, also provides a means of comparing work scheduled with work accomplished. The resulting cost and schedule information allows project managers at both top and intermediate organizational levels to detect problem areas and pinpoint their sources much more readily than would be possible with conventional cost accounting procedures. When followed by appropriate managerial action, such information can lead to effective control of project costs and performance.

The first step in control procedure is the measurement and recording of costs which are incurred as the project progresses. Costs should be coded according to network activities and also organizational function to permit summaries and reports to be made on either basis. If possible (and it usually is), the cost data should be collected in such a way as to be useful for payroll and other accounting purposes.

At the same time costs are reported, an estimate should be made of the percentage of work accomplished. Thus, an activity may have incurred, say, 60 per cent of its budgeted costs but be only 40 per cent completed. If the assumption of a linear relationship between costs and time is valid, such an activity would appear to be heading for an overrun in costs. If such an assumption is in error for certain activities, then they should be broken into separate activities for which the assumption is more reasonable, as noted above, or else estimates should be made of the cost and time remaining for these partially completed nonlinear activities.

Ordinarily, it would be assumed that if 60 per cent of budgeted costs had been spent, then the remaining expenses would amount to no more than 40 per cent of budgeted costs and similarly for time spent and time remaining. Of course, it is not unusual for revisions of original cost and time estimates to be made, as additional information and experience is gained during the course of the project, or as unanticipated problems are encountered. Such revisions can be incorporated in updated budgets and time schedules for purposes of managerial control.

Graphic Displays of Cost and Time Data

With the above cost and time data collected from period to period as the project progresses, some very useful graphic reports may be produced that help managers to answer such questions as:

○ Is the project on schedule? When is the expected completion time?
○ How far over budget are present costs?
○ What are the sources of delay and cost overruns? Is a particular activity in trouble or is some department problem affecting several activities?

Answers to most of these questions may be drawn directly from the graphic display; others may require some investigation, the necessity and direction of which are suggested by the display.

For example, assume that the initial planning phase of a project has led to the total cost budget and time schedule illustrated by solid line A in Figure 6–4. This is essentially a plot of cumulative costs corresponding to a particular schedule of activity start times, as discussed above. Note that the project is scheduled to begin in January, 1970, and to end by the first of April, 1971, with a total cost of $6 million. Assume, further, that the project has been underway for some time and that the current date is marked by the vertical line labeled "Today."

Actual costs expended on the project are plotted as dashed line B, indicating that expenditures have exceeded the budgeted rate of line A. Of and by itself this fact is not particularly helpful. It may be that the project is proceeding ahead of schedule and that the higher costs are merely a reflection of this. On the other hand, if the project is just on schedule or—worse yet—behind schedule in terms of work accomplished, then a definite overrun of costs has occurred. We need to know, then, what work has been completed, in terms of dollars budgeted for this work. Dotted line C displays this information. It represents the value of work completed, measured on the basis of the original cost estimates.

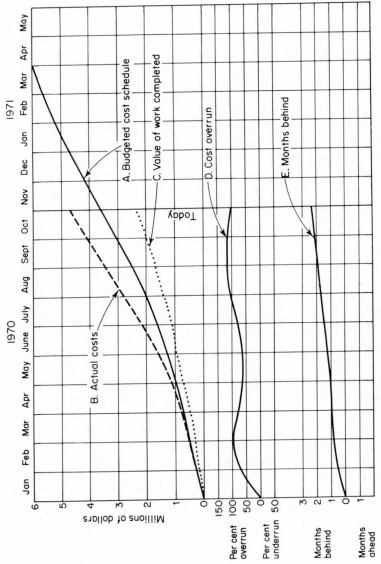

FIGURE 6-4. Schedules of Budgeted versus Actual Costs and Work

The fact that curve C is below curve B indicates that there is an overrun in costs.[5] The amount of overrun at any point in time is represented by the vertical distance between the two curves. Thus at the present time, actual costs ($4.7 million) exceed the value of work completed ($2.4 million) by $2.3 million, an overrun of some 95 percent. Curve D in the smaller graph in the lower left part of Figure 6–4 is a running calculation of the per cent overrun (or underrun, if it occurs), obtained by the formula:

$$\% \text{ Overrun (underrun)} = \frac{(\text{Actual Cost}) - (\text{Value of Work Completed})}{(\text{Value of Work Completed})}$$

(A negative result indicates an underrun.)

In our particular example, curve C also falls beneath curve A, indicating that the project is behind schedule. The amount of this delay at a particular time point is the *horizontal* distance between curve C at that time point and curve A. For example, at the "present time" (November 1st), work valued at $2.4 million has been completed. That same amount of work was originally scheduled to have been completed about the third week in August. Thus, we are about $2\frac{1}{4}$ months behind schedule. Curve E at the bottom of Figure 6–4 is a running tally of the number of months behind. It indicates that the project progressively has fallen further and further behind schedule and that initial delays are not being erased by an accelerated pace on subsequent work but are being further compounded.

A manager facing a situation like that in our hypothetical example would obviously have serious problems to worry about. After only 10 months, the project is already more than 2 months behind schedule and costs are almost double what they should be for the work accomplished. With the project due date rapidly approaching, the manager's immediate concern will probably be how soon the project can be completed and at what cost. Projection of the curves into future months should help to answer these questions for him. Figure 6–5 illustrates such projections. Curve F is an extension of curve B and shows the estimated costs necessary to complete the project. These estimates could be drawn directly from the budgeted costs for the activities not yet completed, or they may be modified according to additional information or experience received since the first estimates were made.

Curve G extends curve C to a new completion date and represents a cost budget based on a revised time schedule of activities yet to be per-formed. The schedule may be based on the original time estimates, or these, too, may be modified as necessary. As with curve A, costs are based on those originally budgeted so that a comparison may be continued between bud-geted and anticipated actual costs. The vertical distance between F and G is a projection of cost overruns. Expressed as a per cent of budget cost, it

[5]Similarly an underrun would result in curve C being above curve B.

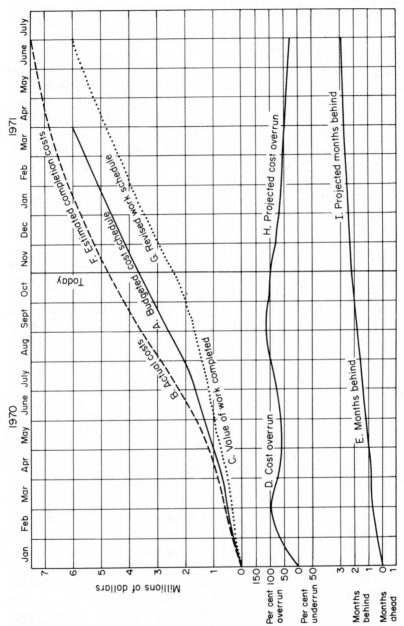

FIGURE 6-5. Projections of Cost Budgets and Work Schedules

93

appears as curve H, an extension of curve D. Similarly, the horizontal distance between curves G and A represents an estimate of how far the project will continue to be behind or ahead of schedule. This difference is plotted as curve I, Projected Months Behind, an extension of curve E.

The obvious problems in our case example would prompt the manager to examine more detailed reports to determine the source or sources of delay and overruns. Before doing so, however, it would be well for him to check the reasonableness of the summary report, particularly with regard to the curves projected into the future. For example, is it likely that the new estimated completion date will be met? The project is presently $2\frac{1}{4}$ months behind schedule, and the projected completion date is 3 months later than the original due date. Can the delay be reduced by expediting some activities? Is this necessary, or even desirable?

In addition the manager should ask if project actual costs are reasonable. Curve F shows an estimated overrun at completion of $1.5 million but the current overrun is considerably more than that—$2\frac{1}{4}$ million. While estimated additional costs to completion are shown as $2\frac{3}{4}$ million on curve F, the value of work yet remaining is $3\frac{1}{2}$ million (see curve G). Is it likely that the remaining activities can be completed for $3/4 million less than their original budgeted costs, as curve F implies—especially when costs to date are almost 100 per cent overrun? On the face of it, the estimated completion costs of curve F appear overly optimistic. Most managers would be quite skeptical of such estimates. A graphic summary like that in Figure 6–5 would enable a manger to readily detect both wayward performance trends and questionable projections into the future, and to initiate whatever action he deems appropriate.

Cost Curve for Activities and Departments

Project summary curves can clearly signal the existence of cost or schedule problems, but not their source. Less highly aggregated data is needed to detect the specific areas contributing to delays or overruns. Similar cost curves based on major subdivisions of the project and, when appropriate, on departments within the organization can provide this information. Suppose, for example, that our project is the development of a new space vehicle, that the major end-items of the project are structure, propulsion system, guidance and control, and payload, and that the responsible organizational departments are research, engineering, manufacturing, and testing. Suppose, further, that Months Behind and Per Cent Overrun charts for all of these end-items and departments appear as in Figure 6–6.

On the basis of these curves, a manager would observe that guidance and control is the end-item and engineering the department most responsible

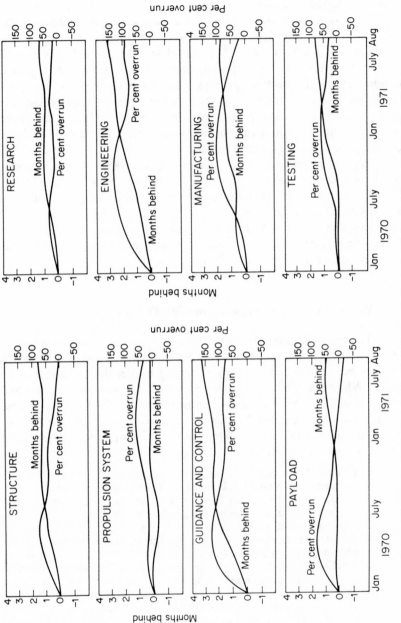

FIGURE 6-6. "Months Behind" and "Per Cent Overrun" Charts for Major End-Items and for Departments

for project overrun and schedule delay. To pinpoint the problem, guidance and control should be broken into smaller subdivisions, down to the level of work packages if necessary. Then it will become apparent whether the problem is general, affecting several subsystems, or whether one or two activities are the source of most of the problems. If the problem is general to the whole system or to much of it, then the manager might suspect a common source of the problem, perhaps traceable to the department responsible. In this case since engineering shows an overrun in budgeted costs, it should be subjected to further scrutiny. Cost curves similar to the above drawn up for subdivisions of engineering should reveal whether the problem is local or general within the department.

While the specific causes of overruns and delays may not be apparent from the cost curves, their sources may still be determined. The manager will know when to ask questions and of whom. As cost and schedule information is displayed in graphic form, it may be quickly understood and interpreted—much more easily than if it were simply tabulated. Then, without sifting through reams of data, the manager can readily spot problem areas that deserve closer scrutiny and probing.

Possible Accounting Problems with PERT/Cost

The managerial benefits from the PERT/Cost system derive largely from the increased detail with which costs are categorized and reported. As noted above, costs are not only identified by department but also by end-item. While this detail permits closer control of project performance and costs, it is also the cause of some accounting problems. Not the least of these is the additional work naturally required to obtain the greater amount of detail—a major clerical task for large projects. More specific accounting problems include the following:

1. *Indirect Costs* Some project costs are not easily identifiable with end-items or specific work packages. Conventionally, such items are considered to be a form of overhead and allocated according to a variety of sometimes arbitrary rules. In some industries—particularly aerospace—cost reimbursable contracts have created incentives for firms to include as many support-type functions as possible on a direct cost basis that may be charged to the customer. Such overhead-type functions are often handled either by preparing for each such function a single work package which spans the duration of the project or a series of short duration packages. Effort would then have to be made to prepare budgets and record actual costs for these indirect cost items. Another approach is to allocate such costs as reasonably as possible to work packages, but the likely effect would be some lessening in the degree of control of these indirect costs.

2. *Overhead Control* PERT/Cost literature suggests reporting overhead

as a single line item. Since the overhead is a sizable expense in most firms, and since overruns may result from indirect as well as direct costs, it seems desirable to provide some means of exerting better control over overhead. One approach is to divide it into separate categories such as indirect labor, indirect materials, and so on, which can be more closely scrutinized. With careful consideration, part of what is ordinarily grouped in overhead might logically be assigned to work packages. For example, supervisory and management overhead can be associated to a large degree with specific work packages. Remaining indirect charges may be handled as in 1 above.

3. *Material Costs* Frequently, the material requirements for various subsystems within a project are compiled at the same time so that purchase orders may be placed for the total amount of each raw material. The intent is to secure the best possible prices through quantity discounts and to assure the availability of required materials. Provisions for estimated scrappage and other losses are included in the order. Because of the long lead time between engineering's release of material requirements and their eventual use in fabrication, actual costs of materials are often incurred long before work packages in which they are used are scheduled to begin. Since the object of PERT/Cost is to account for costs on the basis of work packages, special provisions must be set up not only to allocate material costs to work packages and to measure costs of excess usage but also to identify material variances soon enough to permit corrective action to be taken. It may be that one set of records is required to provide cash flow data, and another set for control purposes within the PERT/Cost accounting system.

These and other problems in the implementation of PERT/Cost have been identified by analysts.[6] And although work continues in the development of the system, it has already been widely accepted and applied. Its emphasis on more careful relating of costs and end-items, and its ability to predict overruns and delays have generally led to considerable improvements in project cost control.

[6]For a more extensive discussion of these problems, see Larry S. Hill, "Some Cost Accounting Problems in PERT/Cost," *J. Indust. Eng.*, XVII, No. 2 (Feb. 1966).

7

Network scheduling
with limited resources

Until now we have assumed that the only constraints in scheduling an activity—that is, in assigning to it a start and finish date—have been technological in nature. An activity can be started, we have implied, as soon as all of its technological predecessors have been completed. If all activities were scheduled as soon as technologically possible, we would have an early start schedule; either of the PERT or CPM variety. Similarly, by considering successor activities we could create a late start schedule, and if this differs from the early start schedule, there are any number of other schedules we could create by shifting slack jobs back and forth within the limits of their respective slacks. All of these schedules may be generated from only two sets of data: (1) activity precedence relations, as exhibited by a network diagram and (2) activity durations (either expected values based on PERT calculations or optimal durations resulting from CPM procedures).

Implicit in such scheduling procedures is the assumption that the resources required to perform activities are available in unlimited supply, or at least that sufficient resources are available for each activity to be scheduled sometime between its earliest and latest start dates. It is true that, in some instances, estimates for individual activity times are influenced by a consideration of available resources. But such estimates are usually made independently of other activity estimates, and the possible competing claims for the same resources are not explicitly considered. While the assumption of unlimited resources may be justified in some cases, most project managers are faced with the problem of relatively fixed manpower availabilities, a certain number of machines or other pieces of equipment, and—considering money as a resource—a limited budget. Jobs which occur on parallel paths through the network may compete for the same resources, and even though precedence constraints wouldn't prevent their being scheduled simultaneously, a limited supply of resources might force them to be scheduled sequentially.

Consider the small project in Figure 7-1, for example, plotted as a schedule graph with a horizontal time scale.

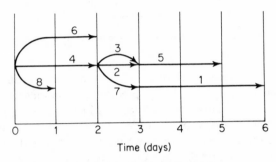

Time (days)

FIGURE 7-1. Schedule Graph, Unlimited Resources

The horizontal length of each activity arrow represents its duration and the number above the arrow, its manpower resource requirement (we'll call it the crew size). Since all the crew sizes are different in this example, we can identify each job by its crew size without confusion. Jobs 4, 6, and 8—all without predecessors—can be scheduled to begin at time 0 by conventional CP calculations, while jobs 2, 3, and 7 can all start at time 2, the second day. Jobs 5 and 1 would follow on the next day. The result is an early start schedule.

Suppose, however, that there are only 10 men available on any one day. Obviously, jobs 4, 6, and 8 cannot all be active at the same time. This applies to jobs 2, 3, and 7 also. To begin the project, either we could schedule job 8 and postpone 6 and 4 until 8 was finished, or vice versa. With respect to jobs 2, 3, and 7, any two of them may be scheduled at the same time, but not all three. A little juggling around with the jobs can lead to the schedule in Fig. 7-2, which is about as good as we can do. Resource requirements do not exceed 10 men on any of the scheduled days, but the completion time has increased from 6 to 7 days. Although there are other feasible schedules, which may be found from a different juggling of jobs, none of them are shorter than that in Figure 7-2. In this case, as frequently happens, the resource limits have resulted in a delayed completion date.

We may observe several things from this exercise. First of all, limited resources result in *practical* problems for the user of critical path scheduling.

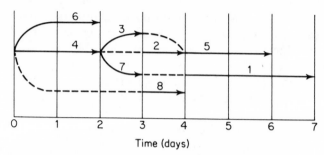

Time (days)

FIGURE 7-2. Schedule Graph, Resource Limit of 10 Men

They impose a whole new set of constraints on the scheduler: Jobs start times are constrained not only by precedence relationships but also by resource availabilities. How does one decide which subset of jobs to schedule on a given day when the whole set of jobs which could start, as far as technological constraints are concerned, would require more than the available resources? This is the first problem we'll look at in this chapter.

Second, limited resources lead to *conceptual* problems in critical path analysis. The usual notions of slack and criticality lose their normal meanings. Notice in Figure 7–2, for instance, that there is no longer a critical path as previously defined—that is, an unbroken sequence of critical jobs from start to finish. Later on in the chapter we shall discuss ways of extending critical path notions to limited resources situations. For now we turn to the practical problems of limited resource scheduling that face the project manager.

The Complexity of Project Scheduling with Limited Resources

Problems of resource scheduling vary in kind and in severity, depending upon the nature of the project and its organizational setting. In some cases there may be just one key resource—perhaps a large crane or a test facility—that is the bottleneck in scheduling a project. Activities must be scheduled so that no two of them requiring the same facility occur at the same time. Or perhaps there is a relatively small number of resources whose limited availability must be jointly considered in scheduling. At the other extreme are projects requiring many resources, most of which are available in fixed, limited amounts. The problem of scheduling activities so that none of the resource availabilities are exceeded and none of the precedence relations are violated is an exceedingly difficult task for projects of even modest size. This is especially true if one tries, simultaneously, to minimize project duration or meet some other reasonable scheduling criteria.

Scheduling projects with limited resources is a type of problem that mathematicians refer to as a large combinatorial problem. That is, there are a very large number of combinations of activity start times—each combination representing a different schedule—too large to enumerate even with a big computer. One can apply linear programming to the problem. (In the Appendix to this chapter, we have formulated an L. P. model of the problem). But even this powerful mathematical tool, aided by the largest and fastest computers, can solve only small projects—those well under 100 activities. Unfortunately, analytical techniques are computationally impractical for most real-life problems of this kind. We need to turn to other approaches.

Heuristic Programs

In recent years a good deal of work has been done in the development of heuristic programs for solving large combinatorial problems. By way of definition, a *heuristic* is a guide or method of reducing search in a problem-solving situation, an aid to the discovery of a solution. The phrase, "rule of thumb," is often used synonymously with "heuristic".

We all use heuristics in solving the countless problems, large and small, that confront us each day. Drawing on our knowledge and experience we devise simple rules of thumb that free us from the task of solving the same or similar problems over and over again. If the problem is how to drive to work in the least time, you might use the rule, "When the freeway is crowded, take the surface street to work." This simple heuristic avoids more complicated problem-solving procedures, such as measuring traffic flows, obtaining highway bulletins, gathering statistical data, and so on. We solve many problems of this kind in the same way. Lacking the time or inclination to pursue more thorough problem-solving procedures, we employ simple (if not infallible) rules of thumb.

Businessmen, likewise, employ heuristics frequently in their own operations. The classic management rule, "Handle only the exceptional problems and let subordinates decide routine matters," is an example in point. While heuristics may not lead to the best solution in each case, experience over a period of time has proved their general usefulness in finding good solutions to recurring problems with a minimum of effort.

In some cases a simple rule of thumb is insufficient. It must be elaborated or combined with other rules to take into account additional factors or exceptional circumstances. A collection of such rules for solving a particular problem is called a *heuristic program*. If sufficiently complex, such a program may require a computer for its solution. Most of the interesting developments in heuristic programming described in recent literature take the form of computer programs. A number of different heuristic programs for scheduling projects with limited resources have been developed in the last few years. Some of these have been outlined in published documents; others, for proprietary reasons, have not.

Heuristic programs for resource scheduling usually take one of two forms:

1. *Resource leveling programs* These attempt to reduce peak resource requirements and smooth out period-to-period assignments, within a constraint on project duration.
2. *Resource allocation programs* These allocate available resources to project activities in an attempt to find the shortest project schedule consistent with fixed resource limits.

We shall discuss these two approaches in greater detail and give examples of programs based on each of them.

Heuristic Methods for Resource Leveling of Project Schedules

In some project situations resources can be acquired or released in practically any desired amounts if one is willing to pay the expenses involved in changing resource levels, such as the costs of hiring, training, unemployment insurance, and so on. It is usually prudent, however, to maintain relatively stable employment levels and to utilize resources at a more constant rate. In such situations resource leveling programs are most appropriate.

For simple projects, or if just one or two key resources are involved, rather informal methods requiring no computer are often quite satisfactory. We suggested earlier that activity slack was a measure of flexibility in the assignment of activity start times. The scheduler may use activity slack as a means of smoothing peak resource requirements. He starts out by calculating an early start schedule for the project and then plotting a resource loading chart for the schedule. In Figure 7-3, for example, the project's early start schedule graph (a) gives rise to the resource loading chart shown in (b). (As before, the number above each arrow represents its resource requirement in the number of men, and since each activity has a different requirement this number can be used to identify the activity as well.)

The peak requirement of 24 men occurs on the third day, when jobs 7, 8, and 9 are all active in the early start schedule. Both 8 and 9 have slack (2 and 7 days, respectively), so these jobs could be delayed up to the amount of their slack without delaying the project completion date. Job 7 is on the critical path, so it seems reasonable to examine the possibilities of moving the other jobs. Since job 9 has the most slack, we are inclined to investigate it first. A look at Figure 7-3 suggests that job 9 could be easily postponed beyond the peak period of day 3 and in fact could be used to help fill up the

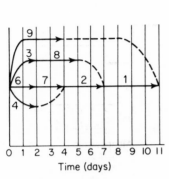

(a) Early start schedule graph

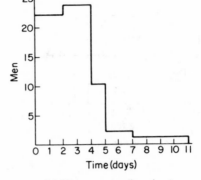

(b) Manpower loading chart

FIGURE 7-3

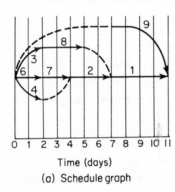

Time (days)

(a) Schedule graph

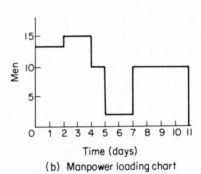

(b) Manpower loading chart

FIGURE 7-4

low point on the loading chart, days 8 through 11. Such a move would yield the graphs of Figure 7–4.

The manpower loading chart has been smoothed considerably, but even further improvement is possible. Days 3 and 4 are peak days now, and of the two jobs active on those days, only job 8 has slack. If we delay job 8 by the full amount of its slack, we obtain the results of Figure 7–5.

The peak period now occurs on days 1 and 2, spanned by jobs 3, 4, and 6. Job 6 is critical, but both 3 and 4 have two days of slack. The best results are obtained by delaying job 3, as shown in Figure 7–6.

At this point, if not sooner, it becomes obvious that we have concocted an example that gives us very nice results: the ideal, completely flat manpower loading chart. For the duration of this project, we would have

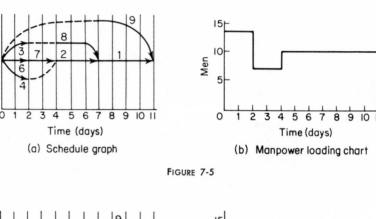

(a) Schedule graph (b) Manpower loading chart

FIGURE 7-5

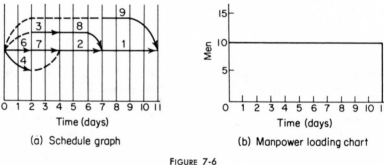

(a) Schedule graph (b) Manpower loading chart

FIGURE 7-6

no need to incur costs for changing resource levels. Real-life projects, of course, could rarely be smoothed with such notable success, but the approach taken in this imaginary project could be used and has been, by many project schedulers.

For larger and more complex projects, hand-smoothing by juggling slack jobs can be very difficult and time consuming. Just drawing and redrawing the charts can be a tedious task as the number of jobs increases. If there were several resources to level, not only would there be more loading charts to keep track of but also the technological interrelations of jobs would make simultaneous smoothing of all resources a tricky proposition. One might find that delaying a slack job would reduce a peak requirement for resource A but result in new peak requirements for resources B and C, due to the shifts in jobs which succeed the initial one. The ramifications of a single move in a project with many interconnecting activities are difficult to anticipate and tedious to trace out by hand methods.

A computer can be used to good advantage at this point, however. Several heuristic-type computer programs have been written; their object is to smooth resource requirements by shifting slack jobs beyond periods of peak requirements.[1] Some of these essentially replicate what a human scheduler would do if he had enough time; others make use of unusual devices or procedures designed especially for the computer. All of them, of course, depend for their success on the tremendous speed and capabilities of electronic computers.

Example of a Resource Leveling Program

One example of such a program and the heuristics upon which it is based is the MS[2] (for multi-ship, multi-shop) workload smoothing program, designed orginally to smooth manpower requirements in naval shipyards.[2] Each ship needing repairs represents a separate project, whose numerous jobs to be completed can be represented in network form. Since several ships may be worked on at one time and each requires men drawn from several shops or skill groups, the problem is essentially one of multiple project scheduling with limited resources (hence the name "multi-ship, multi-shop"). Obviously, such types of problems are not limited to shipyards; they frequently arise in industrial and other settings.

As is true in many project operations, manpower requirements for any one shop in a shipyard may vary greatly from day to day, depending on the arrival of jobs and how big they are. Since shop crew sizes generally must be sufficient to meet maximum manpower requirements, a schedule which reduces peak loads by increasing usage during slack periods would allow smaller shop sizes and hence reduce labor expense. The MS[2] program attempts to do this by scheduling all jobs at their earliest start times and then shifting some of them that occur during peak periods to later slack periods.

First of all an early start schedule, along with total slack values for all jobs, is calculated by regular network procedures. A manpower loading chart is then generated, showing day-by-day manpower requirements in each of the shops for the early start schedule. The program then sets "trigger levels," or resource limits, one unit (man) below the peak requirements in each of the shops, and it attempts to reschedule the jobs so that peak requirements do not exceed the trigger levels. Jobs are then reloaded, or rescheduled, one at a time, until the trigger level is exceeded in some shop. All jobs active on the peak day in that shop are examined, and those which

---

[1]See, for example, A. R. Burgess and J. B. Killebrew, "Variation in Activity Level on a Cyclical Arrow Diagram," *J. Indust. Eng.*, 13 (March-April 1962); L. De Witte, "Manpower Leveling of PERT Networks," *Data Processing for Science/Engineering*, 2, No. 2 (1964), 29; R. C. Wilson, "Assembly Line Balancing and Resource Scheduling," University of Michigan Summer Conference, Production and Inventory Control (1964).

[2]F. K. Levy, G. L. Thompson, and J. D. Wiest, "Multi-Ship, Multi-Shop, Workload Smoothing Program," *Naval Research Logistics Quarterly*, 9, No. 1 (March, 1962).

lack sufficient slack to be shifted beyond the peak period are discarded from consideration. Of those which remain, one is chosen at random and re-scheduled to start at some point beyond the peak day.[3]

Such a move, of course, may affect the early start dates and total slack of jobs following the one moved. These are recalculated and the loading is continued until all jobs are loaded or until the trigger level is again exceeded and another job is shifted. If the trigger levels of each shop are met, then all of them are reduced one unit again, and the process of loading and shifting is repeated.

Should it be impossible for the peaks to be reduced below the trigger levels in one or more shops, then the previous feasible set of trigger levels is called back and the trigger levels are examined on a shop-by-shop basis, starting with the shop with the highest average hourly pay. The trigger level of that shop is lowered, one unit at a time, until no further reduction is possible. Then the next most expensive shop is examined and the trigger levels reduced to the lowest feasible point. This operation is repeated until no trigger levels can be further reduced and a final schedule is reached.

The trigger level can be looked upon as a ceiling pressing down on the manpower requirements. Peaks are reduced by pushing them to the right, as shown in Figure 7-7, parts a and b. The ideal schedule would result in a rectangle, as in part c, but because of fixed sequencing of jobs, variations in crew sizes on different jobs, and the interactions of trigger levels in various shops, the ideal is improbable. It is possible, as we noted earlier, that reducing a peak on one day by shifting a job to the right may result in a second—and perhaps worse—peak later on, in the same shop or in a different one.

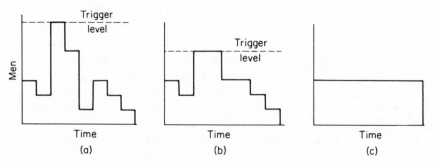

FIGURE 7-7. Smoothing Peak Resource Requirements

[3] There are two elements of randomness here—in the selection of a job from the eligibility list and in the determination of the number of days beyond the peak period that the job is shifted. The probability of an eligible job being chosen is inversely proportional to its manpower requirement, and there is a higher probability of a job being moved a minimum distance beyond the peak rather than a maximum distance, as limited by the job's total slack.

Because of the random elements in the program, schedules produced by repeated applications of the program will likely differ from each other. From a set of such schedules generated and evaluated by the computer, the best schedule can be readily chosen—that is, the schedule requiring the least resources.

It is of interest to note the differences between the heuristics of this type of computer program and those followed in the example represented by Figures 7–3 through 7–6. In the hand-solution, we made use of the human's ability to take a comprehensive look at a manpower loading chart and to detect particular jobs and peak days that could be shifted to "fill up some hole" elsewhere in the schedule. It is quite difficult to program a computer, however, to do the same thing. What a human grasps at a glance, and the cognitive processes he goes through in picturing a shift in jobs, are not easily reduced to a step-by-step program of heuristic rules. Thus, in the computer scheduling model, we resort to more crude trial-and-error search and to random actions, hoping that the speed of the computer and its ability to rapidly generate many schedules will make up for its lack of human capabilities. Of course, as projects grow larger, the human's advantage dwindles with his ability to perceive the project schedule as a whole. The amount of information to process becomes too great, and the computer's relative value increases. What is humanly possible and desirable for small projects becomes infeasible for large ones.

Heuristic Methods for Resource Allocation in Project Scheduling

For many project managers the resource scheduling problem is not only one of smoothing requirements but it is also one of allocating resources that are available only in fixed or relatively fixed amounts. The manager may have a limited staff of skilled design engineers or other difficult-to-replace, skilled personnel, or there may be some fixed number of certain machines or pieces of equipment, or perhaps some construction material can be obtained only at a limited rate. Frequently too, there are budget restrictions. Even if resources could readily be purchased in unlimited quantities, the funds to do so may be limited to certain monthly allowances. As a result, activities can be scheduled only as necessary resources become available, even if the effect is to delay the project completion date.

A modification of the MS^2 program just described conceivably could generate a schedule to satisfy fixed resource limits: You would have to remove the constraint of a fixed due date and push down on the trigger levels until peak requirements were all under the resource limits. If the limits are rather confining, it is likely that many jobs will be squeezed to the right on the schedule chart, delaying the project due date. You can't have constraints both on resource limits and on the project due date.

While such an extension of resource leveling techniques is possible, it isn't very practical, for this reason: If the resource limits are tight, then there will be considerable scheduling and rescheduling of jobs. As the trigger levels are lowered, jobs on peak days will be squeezed to the right, causing all successor jobs to be rescheduled also. Rather than schedule all jobs at early start and then reschedule them repeatedly until resource restrictions are met, it seems more reasonable to generate a feasible schedule to begin with and minimize the subsequent adjustments. This can be done by scheduling jobs each day only up to the limit of resources and then postponing any remaining jobs until resources are sufficient for scheduling them.

Most resource allocation programs are of this type. Resources are allocated on a period-by-period basis to some subset of the available jobs— those whose predecessors have been completed. The essential heuristics of such programs are those that determine *which* jobs shall be scheduled and *which* shall be postponed in any period. The most obvious approach is to use job slack as a basis of priority, scheduling first the jobs which are most critical. In one form or another, this heuristic appears in most of the existing resource allocation programs, in combination with various other rules or modifying heuristics.

A Simple Heuristic Program

As an illustration of the resource allocation approach to project scheduling, consider the simple program shown in flow diagram form in Figure 7–8.[4] The program is based essentially on three rules (heuristics):

1. Allocate resources serially in time. That is, start on the first day and schedule all jobs possible, then do the same for the second day, and so on.
2. When several jobs compete for the same resources, give preference to the jobs with the least slack.
3. Reschedule noncritical jobs, if possible, in order to free resources for scheduling critical or nonslack jobs.

To illustrate how these heuristics operate in the program, let us apply them to a small project consisting of ten jobs, each of which requires a certain amount of time and a given number of men (crew). For simplicity, let us assume that all the men are interchangeable. In practical situations, however, the various jobs may require men of different skills as well as other resources such as machines, materials, money, and so forth.

Figure 7–9 shows the schedule graph for this small project. All jobs have been started as early as their predecessors will allow. The number above each arrow identifies the job and its crew size. Job 4, for example,

---

[4]The illustration in this section is adapted from J. D. Wiest's "Heuristic Programs for Decision Making," *Harvard Business Review* (Sept.-Oct. 1966). Used by permission of *Harvard Business Review*.

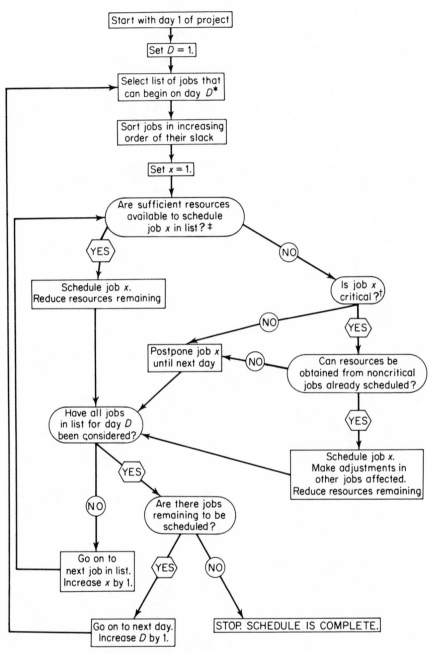

```
            ┌──────────────────────────┐
            │ Start with day 1 of project │
            └──────────────────────────┘
                       │
                 ┌──────────┐
                 │ Set D = 1.│
                 └──────────┘
                       │
            ┌──────────────────────────┐
            │ Select list of jobs that   │
            │ can begin on day D*        │
            └──────────────────────────┘
                       │
            ┌──────────────────────────┐
            │ Sort jobs in increasing    │
            │ order of their slack       │
            └──────────────────────────┘
                       │
                 ┌──────────┐
                 │ Set x = 1.│
                 └──────────┘
```

Are sufficient resources available to schedule job x in list? ‡

YES

NO

Schedule job x. Reduce resources remaining

Is job x critical?†

NO

YES

Postpone job x until next day

NO

Can resources be obtained from noncritical jobs already scheduled?

YES

Have all jobs in list for day D been considered?

Schedule job x. Make adjustments in other jobs affected. Reduce resources remaining

YES

NO

Are there jobs remaining to be scheduled?

YES

NO

Go on to next job in list. Increase x by 1.

Go on to next day. Increase D by 1.

STOP. SCHEDULE IS COMPLETE.

*Day D is the day under consideration.
† A job is <u>critical</u> if it has no slack.
‡Job x is the job under consideration.

FIGURE 7-8

109

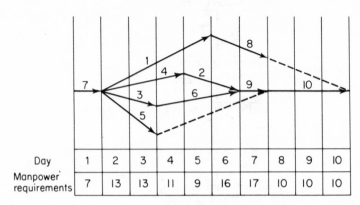

Day	1	2	3	4	5	6	7	8	9	10
Manpower requirements	7	13	13	11	9	16	17	10	10	10

FIGURE 7-9. Schedule Graph, Unlimited Resources

requires 4 men on each of days 2, 3, and 4. Thus, we can calculate daily manpower requirements for the schedule by summarizing vertically the crew sizes of all jobs active on a given day. In the schedule graph in Figure 7–9, manpower requirements start at 7 on day 1, climb to 13 on days 2 and 3, and so on.

Suppose, however, that only 10 men are available for the project on any one day. How should the project be scheduled so as not to exceed this constraint but still to complete the project as soon as possible? One way to find the shortest feasible schedule would be to enumerate all possible schedules. For example, on day 1 there is just one possible choice of jobs (job 7). On day 2, with four jobs available, there are thirteen feasible combinations: four consisting of a single job, six consisting of pairs of jobs, and three consisting of triples of jobs. (The remaining combinations exceed the manpower limit of 10.) Each of these thirteen choices represents a different way to begin a schedule, and multiple choices fan out from each of these on succeeding days. The number of all possible schedules is very large, even for this small project.

Day-to-Day Decisions

The heuristic program diagrammed in Figure 7–8 doesn't examine all possible schedules; it selects just one combination of jobs for each day, only occasionally retracing its steps to see if a better set could be found. Scheduling day by day (as required by the first heuristic of the program—see p. 108), the program would make the following decisions:

Day 1

Only one job (7) is available to start in this period and there are sufficient men to schedule it.

Schedule job 7 (slack = 0, calculated relative to jobs on the critical path, which are defined as having no slack); 3 men remain available.

Day 2

Four jobs (1, 3, 4, and 5) can be started on day 2, but there are not enough men to schedule them all. The second heuristic calls for scheduling the jobs with the least slack first.

Schedule job 3 (slack = 0); 7 men remain.
Schedule job 4 (slack = 0); 3 men remain.
Schedule job 1 (slack = 3); 2 men remain.

Job 5 must be delayed, as there are just 2 men unassigned.

Postpone job 5 (slack = 4).

Day 3

We assume that jobs cannot be interrupted once started; partially completed jobs have first call on the available resources.

Continue job 3 (slack = 0); 7 men remain.
Continue job 4 (slack = 0); 3 men remain.
Continue job 1 (slack = 3); 2 men remain.

Since there are still not enough men for job 5, it must be delayed again.

Postpone job 5 (slack = 3).

At this point the schedule graph appears as shown in Figure 7–10. Heavy lines indicate jobs already scheduled; light lines are projected schedules, which still must be checked for feasibility. Note that job 5, which has been postponed two days, now has only two days slack, or possible slippage, remaining.

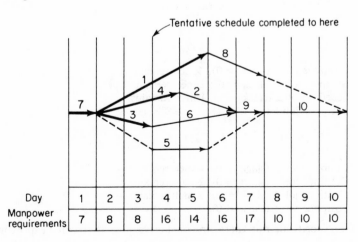

Day	1	2	3	4	5	6	7	8	9	10
Manpower requirements	7	8	8	16	14	16	17	10	10	10

FIGURE 7-10

Day 4

>Continue job 4 (slack = 0); 6 men remain.
>Continue job 1 (slack = 3); 5 men remain.
>Job 6 has no slack and hence is critical, but only 5 men are still unassigned.

The third heuristic is now brought into play: Are there noncritical jobs still active which could be postponed without delaying the project? Job 1 satisfies this requirement and hence is reassigned to begin later.

>Reschedule job 1; 6 men remain.
>Schedule job 6 (slack = 0); 0 men remain.
>Postpone job 5 (slack = 2).

The schedule graph at the end of day 4 is shown in Figure 7–11.

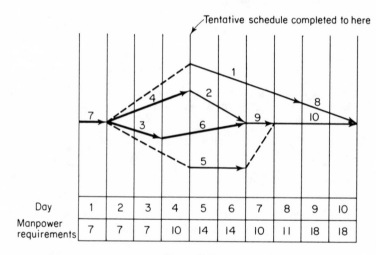

Figure 7-11

Day 5

>Continue job 6 (slack = 0); 4 men remain.
>Schedule job 2 (slack = 0); 2 men remain.
>Schedule job 1 (slack = 0); 1 man remains.
>Postpone job 5 (slack = 1).

Day 6

>Continue job 6 (slack = 0); 4 men remain.
>Continue job 2 (slack = 0); 2 men remain.
>Continue job 1 (slack = 0); 1 man remains.
>Postpone job 5 (slack = 0).

Job 5 is now critical, but there are no active jobs that can be postponed

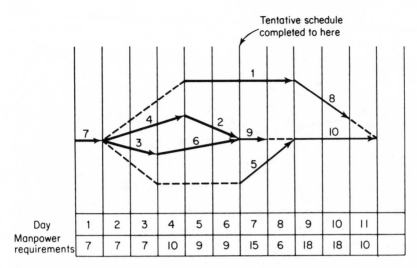

Tentative schedule
completed to here

Day	1	2	3	4	5	6	7	8	9	10	11	
Manpower requirements	7	7	7	10	9	9	15	6	18	18	10	

FIGURE 7-12

without delaying the project. Note that the projected finish date is delayed a day by job 5's postponement, as shown in Fig. 7–12.

Day 7

> Continue job 1 (slack = 1); 9 men remain.
> Schedule job 5 (slack = 0); 4 men remain.
> Postpone job 9 (slack = 1).

Day 8

> Continue job 5 (slack = 0); 5 men remain.
> Postpone job 9 (slack = 0); no noncritical jobs can be rescheduled.
> Postpone job 8 (slack = 2).

At the end of day 8, the schedule graph appears as in Figure 7–13.

Remaining Period

Program decisions for the remaining six days are as follows:

> *Day 9*—Schedule job 9 (slack = 0); 1 man remains. Postpone job 8 (slack = 2).
> *Day 10*—Schedule job 10 (slack = 0); no men remain. Postpone job 8 (slack = 1).
> *Day 11*—Continue job 10 (slack = 0); no men remain. Postpone job 8 (slack = 0).
> *Day 12*—Continue job 10 (slack = 1); no men remain. Postpone job 8 (slack = 0).

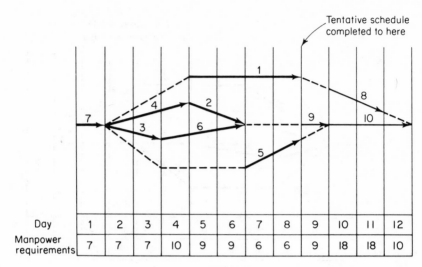

FIGURE 7-13

Day 13—Schedule job 8 (slack = 0); 2 men remain.
Day 14—Continue job 8 (slack = 0); 2 men remain.

All jobs are now scheduled. The final schedule graph appears in Figure 7–14.

Thus the manpower limit of 10 men per day has resulted in a four-day increase in the project length, compared with the unlimited resources schedule. In this application the heuristic program has found an optimal

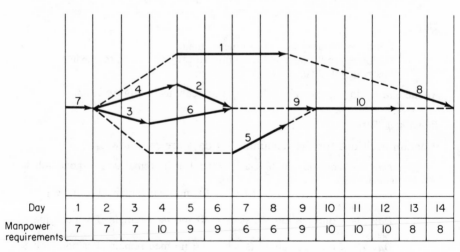

FIGURE 7-14. Final Schedule—Limited Resources

schedule. There are other feasible schedules, but none is shorter than fourteen days.

It would not be difficult to think up sample projects for which the above program would *not* produce optimum results. Of course, no heuristic program can *guarantee* an optimum schedule, but the above program could be considerably improved by the addition of appropriate heuristics which take into account more information or special circumstances. For instance, it may be possible in some projects to crash or stretch out certain jobs by varying the rate of resource application. Also, some jobs might allow *splitting* —that is, an interruption in their schedule—while others may have to move to completion once started. Resource limits themselves may vary from period to period. An operational scheduling program should take cognizance of these and other factors in order to be generally useful for project scheduling. Project scheduling situations often differ so markedly, however, that special programs must be written or more general programs modified to meet particular needs. Heuristic programming, as a general technique, facilitates such custom tailoring of scheduling procedures.

The SPAR-1 Resource Allocation Model

A number of different resource allocation programs for scheduling large projects have been described in published accounts.[5] One of these, called SPAR-1,[6] illustrates how the basic model that has been discussed can be elaborated with additional heuristics. A brief description of its structure is given here for the reader who is interested in such programs and who might be stimulated to try his own hand at heuristic programming. The basic logic of a heuristic scheduling program can be worked out by someone who knows little or nothing about computer programming per se.

[5]See, for example, J. Moshman, J. Johnson, and Madalyn Larsen, "RAMPS: A Technique for Resource Allocation and Multiproject Scheduling," Proceedings of the 1963 Spring Joint Computer Conference; R. L. Martino, *Project Management and Control Vol. III, Resource Allocation and Scheduling* (New York: American Management Association, 1965); J. E. Kelley, Jr., "The Critical Path Method: Resources Planning and Scheduling," Chapt. 21 in *Industrial Scheduling*, (eds.) J. F. Muth and G. L. Thompson (Englewood Cliffs, N. J.: Prentice-Hall, Inc., 1963); J. J. Moder and C. R. Phillips, *Project Management with CPM and PERT* (New York: Reinhold Publishing Corp., 1964); P. C. Hooper, "Resource Allocation and Levelling," Proceedings of the Third CPA Symposium, Operational Research Society, London (1965); T. L. Pascoe, "An Experimental Comparison of Heuristic Methods for Allocating Resources," Ph. D. thesis, Cambridge University Engineering Depart., 1965. Many other models have been developed by companies primarily for their own use. U. S. Steel and Richfield Oil, for example, have written programs discussed in private documents; but detailed descriptions of the programs have not yet appeared in generally available publications.

[6]For "Scheduling Program for Allocating Resources," see J. D. Wiest, "A Heuristic Model for Scheduling Large Projects with Limited Resources," *Mgt. Science*, **13**, No. 6 (Feb. 1967), B359–B377.

In a manner similar to that of the simple model described earlier, SPAR-1 allocates available resources, period by period, to project jobs listed according to their early start times. Jobs are scheduled, starting with the first period, by selecting from the list of those currently available and sorted in order of their total slack (which is based on technological constraints only and normal resource assignments). The most critical jobs have the highest probability of being scheduled first, and as many of these jobs are scheduled as available resources permit. If an available job fails to be scheduled in that period, an attempt is made to schedule it the next period. Eventually, all jobs so postponed become critical and move to the top of the priority list of available jobs.

This basic program is modified by a number of additional scheduling heuristics or subroutines generally designed to increase the use of available resources and/or to decrease the length of the schedule. For simplicity in our description of these heuristics, we will refer to "resources" as "men," to the "amount of resources applied to a job" as the "crew size," to a "group of homogeneous resources" as a "shop," and to the "scheduling period" as a "day." Any other units, of course, could be used in place of these.

Crew Size: With each job is associated a normal crew size, or the number of men or other resources normally assigned to the job; a maximum crew size, or the maximum number of men required for crashing the job; and a minimum crew size, or the smallest number of men which can be assigned to the job. Normally, these three crew sizes will differ from each other. But in some cases two or all three of them may be equal, when jobs cannot be stretched out or crashed. The rules for crew size selection are as follows: If a job to be scheduled is critical (the degree of criticality is specified by an input parameter), it is placed on a priority list and given special treatment. If sufficient men are available, the job is scheduled at its maximum crew size; that is, it is crashed. If insufficient men are available to do so, or even to schedule the job at normal crew size, then an attempt is made to obtain the required men by means of the borrow and reschedule routines which we describe below. If all efforts fail, however, and the job cannot be scheduled even at minimum crew size, then its early start date is delayed one period, and an attempt is made to schedule the job on the following day. Jobs with sufficient positive slack (that is, noncritical jobs) are scheduled at normal crew size if the required number of men are available; but if resources available are insufficient for scheduling even the minimum crew size, then the jobs are delayed for consideration until the next day.

Augment Critical Jobs: Repeated attempts are made to speed up critical jobs—including those which become critical after being scheduled— which have crew sizes less than their maximum crew size. Before any new jobs are scheduled on a given day, jobs previously scheduled and still active are examined. If any of these is critical and has a crew size less than its maximum, and if resources are available, the job's crew size is increased as much as possible up to the maximum.

Multi-resource Jobs: Sometimes a job requires a number of different resources, such as men of different skills, machines, money, and so on, each of which may be limited in quantity. For such multi-resource jobs, separate jobs are created for each resource and the jobs are constrained to start on the same day with the same level of resource assignment—that is, normal, minimum, or maximum crew size.

Borrow from Active Jobs: If resources available are insufficient for scheduling some critical job j, then the model enters into a procedure for searching currently active jobs to see if sufficient men might be borrowed from them for scheduling job j on that day. Men are borrowed from a job only when the resultant stretching of the job will not delay the entire project.

Reschedule Active Jobs: Sometimes a critical job j could be scheduled if other jobs previously scheduled which use the same resources had been postponed to a later time. The model scans the list of currently active jobs and picks out those which could be postponed without delaying the project due date. If sufficient men could be obtained in this way and/or from the borrow routine described earlier, then job j is scheduled and the necessary adjustments are made in previous assignments. (This is similar to the third heuristic of our simple model on p. 108.)

The reschedule routine has much the same effect as a "look-ahead" feature. Instead of attempting to look ahead to future needs of critical jobs (which would be difficult to do in the limited resource case, since jobs are not always scheduled at their early start), SPAR-1 schedules all jobs possible as it moves along from day to day. It repents, so to speak, of previous scheduling errors if jobs are encountered which have more critical need of resources than the jobs to which the resources were assigned at earlier dates.

Add on Unused Resources: After as many jobs as possible are scheduled on a given day, there still may be unused resources in some of the shops for that day. The model compiles a list of active jobs to which these resources might be assigned (that is, jobs which require these resources and which have assigned crew sizes less than the maximum crew size possible). It arranges these jobs in ascending order of their total slack. Proceeding down the list, the model increases the crew size of these jobs until the unused resources or the list of jobs is exhausted. The increment, however, is temporary; jobs supplemented in this way return to their assigned crew size the next day, unless unused resources are also available then.

After going through the above scheduling routines each day, SPAR-1 records the results in a manpower loading table which notes the number of men assigned on each job and in each shop, and it updates the critical path data—that is, the early and late start times, early and late finish times, and total slack. Note that several of the above routines may alter a job's criticality; for example, when the maximum crew size is assigned to a critical job, the shortening of the job may result in its gaining positive slack and perhaps some other job or jobs becoming critical.

SPAR-1 is able to accommodate single or multiple projects, variable crew sizes, jobs that can be split, variable shop limits, shift or nonshift scheduling, and various criteria functions for evaluating a schedule. Probabilistic elements in the program can lead to different schedules with successive applications of the program (in a manner similar to MS²). The best of several schedules can then be selected. Currently written in FORTRAN IV for a 32K machine, SPAR-1 is dimensioned to handle a project with up to 1,200 jobs, 1,000 nodes, and 25 shops. Another version of the model written for a larger computer allows projects up to 6,000 jobs to be scheduled.

Various adaptions of the model have been made for application to particular scheduling problems. For example, in one situation, some jobs could be processed only on machine A, others on machine B, and still others on either of the machines. For the latter group of jobs, the model selects the machine that has idle time, if any, and adjusts the job durations according to the machine chosen (A and B differ in their efficiency). Other changes are also possible. The reader very likely can think of scheduling problems, perhaps drawn from his own experience, that would require modifications in the model or perhaps the writing of an entirely new program.

A number of different and interesting approaches have been taken by several authors of heuristic scheduling programs. RAMPS, for example, has a rather elaborate set of heuristics for choosing jobs to be scheduled on a given day. Not only is job slack considered but also such factors as work continuity, cost of idle resources, number of successors to an eligible job, and several others, all of which are given weights to reflect their relative importance. All feasible schedules for each scheduling period are examined, and the one is chosen which rates highest by the above weighted criteria factors.

We note again that no heuristic program can promise to yield an optimal project schedule—optimal by such criteria as resource usage, minimum project length, and so on. In fact, it would be impossible in most cases to determine if a given schedule *is* optimal. Analytic procedures, on the other hand, can guarantee such results. Various approaches have been formulated—including linear programming, integer programming, electrical network theory, branch-and-bound techniques, dynamic programming, and others—but none of them are feasible, as yet, for anything but very small projects. For the present and forseeable future, heuristic programs offer the most promise for dealing with the problem of scheduling large projects with limited resources.

Conceptual Problems of Critical Path Analysis
When Resources Are Limited

As mentioned earlier, ordinary critical path scheduling techniques do not take explicit account of job resource requirements or of possible limitations on resource availabilities. Implicitly, they assume that the only constraints on the start time of a job are technological; that is, a job can be started as soon as its predecessors have been completed. With every job started as early as possible, a schedule of early start times is created. Similarly, late start times for jobs are established if every job is delayed as

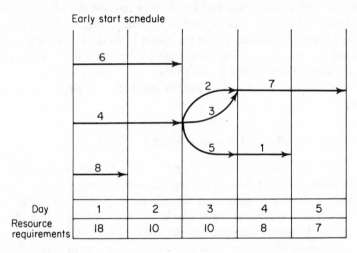

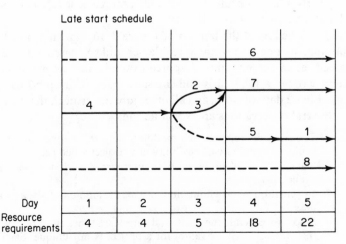

FIGURE 7-15. Schedule Graphs—Unlimited Resources

much as possible, given the constraints of its successors and some final project due date. We defined total slack as the difference between a job's early and late start times. It represents a degree of flexibility allowed the scheduler: A job may be delayed for whatever reason, up to the amount of its total slack without delaying the finish date of the project. To illustrate, Figure 7–15 shows a simple network project in schedule graph form. Once again the identifying number over each arrow represents its resource requirement, say the number of men needed each day for the job. The top diagram is an early start schedule. All jobs are started as early as their precedence relationships permit. The bottom diagram is a late start schedule, with day 5 taken as the due date. No job could start later in this diagram without violating the ordering constraints or delaying the project. In this first example we have assumed unlimited resources, and a job's slack is measured simply as the difference in start times for the job in the two schedules. Thus, job 6 at the top of the diagram has 3 days of slack, jobs 5 and 1 in the middle have 1 day of slack, and job 8 at the bottom has 4 days of slack. All others are slackless.

Slack in a Limited Resource Schedule

Suppose, however, that resources are limited to 10 men a day. Now the jobs requiring 6, 4, and 8 men cannot all begin at the same time. Several schedules are possible, but the one shown at the top of Figure 7–16 is optimal. There is no feasible schedule which is shorter. Note that job 8 is delayed to the fourth day and that the project duration has been increased to six days. Since no job could be started earlier, given the precedence relationships *and* resource constraints, this represents an early start schedule in the case of limited resources. Unlike the unlimited resource case, which had a unique early start schedule, this limited resource schedule is only one of several possible early start schedules.

The schedule at the bottom of Figure 7–16, similarly, is a late start schedule (again, one of several possible schedules), based on a due date of 6. Slack, as in the unlimited resource example, can be measured as the difference between a job's early and late start times. Thus, job 2 has 1 day of slack, job 1 has 2 days of slack, and all other jobs are critical, that is, slackless.

Several observations are worth noting:

1. The slack concept, though modified, may still be used and retains its utility as a measure of flexibility in a project schedule.
2. Slack is dependent upon both precedence orderings *and* resource availability.
3. In general, resource limitations reduce the amount of slack in a schedule.
4. Since, in general, the early and late start schedules are not unique, then the set of slack values for a project is not unique. Slack is *con-*

Early start schedule

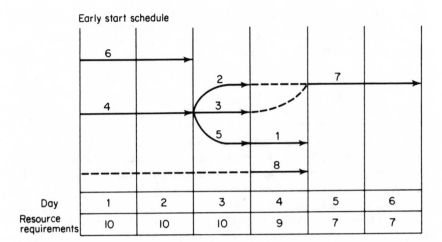

Day	1	2	3	4	5	6
Resource requirements	10	10	10	9	7	7

Late start schedule

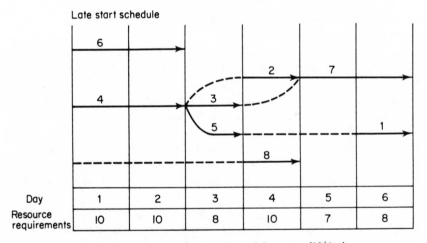

Day	1	2	3	4	5	6
Resource requirements	10	10	8	10	7	8

FIGURE 7-16. Schedule Graphs—Limited Resources (10/day)

ditional upon the scheduling rules for creating early start and late start schedules.

5. While a critical path of technologically connected jobs does not always exist in a limited resource schedule, under certain conditions a "critical sequence" of slackless jobs which span the length of the project can be identified.[7] The jobs are continuous in time, if not in predecessor-

[7]The conditions are described in detail in J. D. Wiest, "Some Properties of Schedules for Large Projects with Limited Resources," *Opns. Res.*, **12**, No. 3 (May-June, 1964).

successor relationship. One such critical sequence may be seen in the early start schedule of Figure 7-16, consisting of jobs 4, 5, 8, and 7. (Jobs 6 and 3 are slackless jobs parallel to 4 and 5, respectively, and could be named in alternate critical sequences.)

The Late Start Schedule

Heuristic programs like SPAR-1 generate, in effect, an early start limited resource schedule. With slight modifications and using the same heuristics, they could also generate late start, limited resource schedules. Or, without modifications, such programs can effect the same results if the network is reversed in its orientation—that is, all jobs have their predecessors and successors reversed[8]—and if scheduling starts with the final day and proceeds backward through time to the first day. Applied in this double fashion, a heuristic program could permit the calculation of limited resource slack, a more reliable measure of schedule flexibility than results from conventional slack calculation.

Value of the Late Start Schedule

The late start schedule has interest beyond its function of permitting the calculation of slack values, however. In many projects the investment of labor and materials in the various activities is quite sizable. If time-adjusted value-of-money concepts are taken into account (as they should be for extended projects), then the late start schedule has a marked advantage. The later one can postpone investments in project jobs, then the lower will be the present value of such investments (and, by summation, the present value of the whole project). A late start schedule would thus result in the lowest present value, and an early start schedule the highest present value, of job-related project costs.

Given this observation, one might ask if all projects should be scheduled according to late start job times. The answer depends upon the degree of uncertainty of job times. If one were virtually certain of the correctness of job time estimates and if there were little chance of unexpected delays, then the late start schedule would usually be the preferable one. Many kinds of projects come close to these requirements, especially when the project is one which has been done before or is similar to an earlier effort. Examples include the construction of tract homes, the manufacture of large hydroelectric generators or diesel locomotives, and the overhauling of jet

[8] A simple transformation of schedule dates is involved. If the schedule is n days long, then day 1 becomes day n, day 2 becomes day $(n-1)$ and in general, day i becomes day $n + 1 - i$.

aircraft engines. In all of these and similar projects, there may be some elements of uncertainty, but reasonably good time estimates can be made for the majority of activities. The time estimates themselves often contain a safety factor to allow for uncertainties. Investments in such projects may be effectively reduced by scheduling activities at or near their late start times.

Projects with Uncertain Activity Estimates

On the other hand, research and development types of projects are characterized by a high degree of uncertainty, not only in the time estimates for activities but also in the activities themselves. It would be risky to schedule such activities at their late start times; as any underestimates of activity times or unforeseen difficulties would directly lead to a delay in the project completion time. Scheduling such activities at their early start times allows the project manager some time cushion, at least for those activities with slack, to absorb delays in activity completion times or to add additional activities whose need was not anticipated at the time of initial scheduling.

Probably most projects have activities, or jobs, of both kinds—those for which time estimates can be accurately made and those which are highly uncertain. Development projects have more of the latter kind, while some construction and manufacturing projects consist mainly of the former kind. This suggests a possible modification of the scheduling heuristics, or at least an option to be used when desired. In place of, or in addition to, job slack as criteria for a priority ordering of jobs to be scheduled, jobs could be characterized by the degree of certainty associated with their time estimate. Those with the greatest uncertainty would receive highest priority for early scheduling; those with more certain time estimates would tend to be scheduled later, or possibly to be postponed up to their late start times.

Planning Versus Scheduling

Several limited resource project scheduling models are presently operational and have demonstrated their worth to managers in a variety of applications. Not only are they useful in generating day-to-day schedules for guiding a firm's project operations, but they have also proved to be valuable planning tools. Long-range schedules, based on expected project requirements and present or planned manpower and equipment capabilities, may be projected into the future. Bottlenecks in certain resources are likely to be uncovered and plans drawn up for relieving such shortages. Various resource patterns may be tried and the resulting schedules compared. Scheduling models may thus be used to simulate long-range operations under various assumed conditions. Such a capability would be especially useful for a company with long lead-times on resource procurement.

Conclusion

The last word is not yet in on project scheduling models. Continued development and experiment on the part of researchers and practitioners will help to measure the worth of various scheduling rules that have been suggested, and, it is hoped, lead to new approaches that are even more effective. We are safe in saying, however, that the heuristic approach to project scheduling, aided by the computational power of a digital computer, has and will continue to contribute in an important way to solving some of the complex planning and scheduling problems of large project management.

A p p e n d i x: *Linear Programming Formulation—*
Project Scheduling With Limited Resources

Linear programming provides an analytic solution to the problem of project scheduling with limited resources. Using an approach similar to Bowman's for the job shop problem,[9] we may develop a project scheduling model as follows:

Subscripts and their ranges:

s shop (resource) $s = 1, 2, \ldots, m$
d day (time period) $d = 1, 2, \ldots, z$
j job (activity) $j = 1, 2, \ldots, n$
p immediate predecessor of j; $p \in P_j$
      = [all immediate predecessors of j]

Variables:

x_{jd} activity of job j on day d; constrained to the integer values 1 (if job j is active) or 0 (if job j is inactive).

Constants:

a_{sd} men available in shop s on day d
c_{sj} crew size; men of shop s required on job j
t_j time length of job j, in days

Constraints:

1. $0 \leq x_{jd} \leq 1$ (and by integer programming techniques, x is constrained to equal either 0 or 1) all j_d

---

[9]E. H. Bowman, "The Schedule–Sequencing Problem," *Operations Research*, **7**, No. 5 (Sept.-Oct., 1959), 621–624.

2. Jobs will be performed:

$$\sum_{d=1}^{z} x_{jd} = t_j, \qquad j = 1, \ldots, n$$

3. Capacity of shop will not be exceeded:

$$\sum_{j=1}^{n} c_{sj} x_{jd} \leq a_{sd}, \qquad d = 1, \ldots, z$$
$$s = 1, \ldots, m$$

4. No job will be started before its predecessors are completed:

$$t_p x_{jd} \leq \sum_{i=1}^{d-1} x_{pi} \qquad \text{all } p \in P_j$$
$$d = 1, \ldots, z$$
$$j = 1, \ldots, n$$

5. No jobs will be split:

$$t_j x_{jd} - t_j x_{j(d+1)} + \sum_{i=d+2}^{z} x_{ji} \leq t_j,$$
$$j = 1, \ldots, n$$
$$d = 1, \ldots, z$$

Objective function:

$$\text{minimize} \qquad 1 \sum_{j=1}^{n} x_{jk} + 4 \sum_{j=1}^{n} x_{j(k+1)} + 16 \sum_{j=1}^{n} x_{j(k+2)}$$

$$+ \ldots + R_z \sum_{j=1}^{n} x_{jz}, \text{ where } k \text{ is some number such that}$$

$0 < k < z$, and $R_z = 4R_{(z-1)}$.

The 4 is somewhat arbitrarily chosen to assure that the model will seek the shortest schedule satisfying the above constraints. Not shown are the additional constraints necessary to assure integer solutions (either 0 or 1) for x_{jd}. We should note, also, that the model does not allow for crashing or stretching a job, nor is allowance made for use of premium cost resources, for example, overtime. In spite of these simplifications, the L. P. problem is a formidable one in terms of sheer size, even for a small project. For example, a project with 55 jobs in 4 shops with a time span of 30 days has 6,870 constraints and 1,650 variables (not counting slack variables or the additional equations and variables necessary to assure an integer solution). Many of these equations, of course, are redundant, and many of the variables could be eliminated at the beginning by calculating the early start times for all jobs, assuming unlimited resources. Then all $x_{jd} = 0$, $1 \leq d \leq$ (early start of j). Nevertheless, for practical size projects even a trimmed-down formulation would probably exceed the capacity of present computers and, in any event, would be an inefficient means of solving the project scheduling problem.

8

Problems and prospects
in applications of CPM/PERT

We have completed our description of the basic PERT/CPM models and some of their extensions. From the viewpoint now of the final chapter, we can appraise these models with a more detached and comprehensive perspective than was possible when we were examining their structure and operation at close range. Now that we know *how* they work, we are in a better position to ask, "Are they as useful as claimed? Do they do what they are supposed to do? Will they really help a project manager to plan and schedule a project?"

These are important questions, and they should be answered before we complete our small book. The models are essentially simple and straight-forward; network calculations, though tedious for large projects, are not complex; and the results follow logically from the assumptions upon which the models are built. However well thought-out the models are, though, we want to know if they are accurate representations of that portion of the real world they attempt to model. No model is any better than the assumptions which underlie it; so a logical place for us to begin our evaluation is with the PERT/CPM assumptions. From a consideration of these, and of how closely they approximate real world conditions, we shall turn to some operational problems of applying PERT and CPM, and note some of the observations and criticisms of practitioners—those who have had experience in applying the models to project management.

The PERT and CPM Assumptions

There are many assumptions, explicit or implicit, which underlie the network models, and our list here is by no means exhaustive. But there are a few which, we believe, are important and relevant to our evaluation here. Not necessarily in order of importance, they include the following:

1. *A project can be subdivided into a set of predictable, independent activities.* ("Independence" here refers to the separateness of the activities in an operational sense, rather than in a time-ordered technological sense. That is, a clear beginning and ending point for each activity can be identified, and activities whose predecessors are completed can be started and stopped independently of each other.)

Two aspects of this assumption have been challenged by observers and practitioners. First is the assumption that activities comprising a project can be known beforehand. While this is not unreasonable for certain projects involving well-established technology and operations, for some projects, such as research and development programs involving state-of-the-art developments, this is not necessarily true. All problems cannot be anticipated in advance; therefore, activities necessary for their solution cannot be planned and included in a project network. To some extent the network must develop or change as the project proceeds. Concerning such projects, Eyring has argued that PERT may even be dysfunctional as a planning model for R & D managers in that the mere attempt to list the activities necessary to complete a research project may tend to remove the flexibility the manager needs to shift directions and procedures as new problems and possibilities arise in the course of the project's completion. The skillful manager, he claims, is not one who can set down a plan and follow it faithfully but one who can rapidly respond to new information as it develops by shifting resources to more promising avenues of endeavor, even if it means scrapping an original plan.[1] To the extent, then, that a project cannot be laid out with reasonable certainty in the planning stage, PERT and CPM are not so useful and appropriate as might be desired.

The second aspect of the assumption concerns the identification of separate independent activities. In practice, while the assumption is often valid, not all activities can be so clearly identified. Where one activity ends and another begins is sometimes a matter of arbitrary choice, and some functions necessary for a project, such as the general management function

[1] Henry B. Eyring, "Evaluation of Planning Models for Research and Development Projects," (D.B.A. thesis, Harvard University, June, 1963). In his thesis Eyring presents an interesting and thoughtful analysis of both conceptual and practical problems encountered in applying network planning models to R & D projects.

or a support function like legal counsel, fit somewhat awkwardly into the definition of an activity.

Occasionally, also, two activities which appear on separate parallel paths in the network *must* be performed at the same time; they are not operationally independent, in spite of the way they appear on the network.[2]

2. *The precedence relationships of project activities can be completely represented by a noncyclical network graph in which each activity connects directly into its immediate successors.*[3] For many projects, this assumption is valid, but in certain situations it is not. In the first place, not all precedence relationships can be anticipated before a project begins; this is especially true for research and development types of projects which involve new technology and unknown problems. Second, while a network implies a known and fixed ordering of activities, in practice, some precedence relationships (and activities themselves) are contingent upon the outcome of previous activities. For example, if a test phase for a new missile guidance system is successfully completed, the next activity may be to manufacture the system. But if the test fails, the system may go back to the drawing boards. Neither PERT nor CPM allows for *conditional* activities and precedence orderings of this type. All activities in the network *must* be performed, and in the order shown.

Several researchers have attempted to modify the basic models, however, to incorporate the possibility of alternative outcomes of certain events. For each conditional-type activity, probabilities are estimated for each possible outcome. Since only one of the several possible paths leading from the activity is actually followed, a project network with many such activities would consist largely of contingent paths whose activities would never be performed. Though the models have not been widely applied, they are interesting and worthy of review by the manager faced with projects which don't fit the traditional PERT/CPM mold.[4]

<hr/>

[2]Part of this difficulty is due, however, to the problems associated with aggregating large detailed networks. When activities are broken into sufficiently small units of work, then predecessor relationships can be shown with considerable accuracy. But if a "big picture" view of the network is desired, without the clutter of thousands of arrows and nodes, activities must be grouped together into higher level aggregate tasks. Usually, this requires that some of the precedence connections between small tasks be ignored and that only the major technological relationships be retained. Critical path calculations based on aggregate networks may thus be somewhat distorted.

[3]A connection through a dummy activity is still considered direct. By noncyclical, we mean that no part of the network loops back on itself. A loop, or cycle, would exist, for example, if the following precedence relationships were given: Job 1 is a predecessor of job 2, job 2 is a predecessor of job 3, and job 3 is a predecessor of job 1.

[4]See A. A. B. Pritsker and W. W. Rapp, "GERT: Graphical Evaluation and Review Technique, Part I: Fundamentals," *J. Indust. Eng.*, XVII, No. 5 (May, 1966). Part II: "Probabilistic and Industrial Engineering Applications," XVII, No. 6 (June, 1966). For another modification of network models, in which a manager *chooses* between alternative paths which branch from certain nodes of a network, see W. Crowston and G. L. Thompson, "Decision CPM: A Method for Simultaneous Planning, Scheduling and Control of Projects," *Opns. Res.*, **15**, 3 (May-June, 1967), 407–426.

3. *Activity times may be estimated—either as single-point estimates or as three-point PERT estimates—and are independent of each other.* Critical path calculations depend upon given time estimates for all activities. Such calculations, naturally, are only as good as the time estimates upon which they are based; some time estimates may be rather gross if the projects involve new technology or highly uncertain outcomes.[5] The problem is not unique with PERT and CPM, of course; most scheduling methods require time inputs. But PERT and CPM are especially sensitive to these estimates because so much of the output of the models depends upon activity times, for example various slack measures for activities and events, early and late start times for activities and events, identification of the critical path, and the expected mean and variance of activity and project durations.

Also important to PERT/CPM is the assumption of independence of activity durations. Both identification of the critical path and estimation of its length require that durations of critical path activities may be added directly. In practice, however, activity times are not always independent of each other. It is not uncommon for an activity to have to be accelerated as a result of delay in the completion of one or more of its predecessors. Also, as we noted in Chapter 7, resource limitations may cause time dependencies of activities sharing the same resources. Scheduling one activity may cause another otherwise independent activity to be stretched out (or postponed) because of a lack of sufficient common resources.

To some extent, both types of time dependencies may be accounted for in the planning-scheduling phase of project management. With the results of network calculations based on an initial set of time estimates, a manager may examine the path of critical activities and determine if one or more of these might be expedited to shorten the critical path (as discussed in Chapter 3). With these adjustments the network is recalculated, and the process is repeated until a satisfactory schedule is reached. Similarly, if resource conflicts are observed, activity start-times may be adjusted or durations changed along the lines suggested in Chapter 7. In this way, time dependencies are anticipated and planned for before the project begins. Of course, when activities are not performed as planned, then adjustments have to be made as the project proceeds. But, once again, this is not a problem unique to PERT and CPM. Indeed, one of the useful aspects of the models is their ability to *project* the effects of unanticipated delays as these are encountered, and thus to guide managers in making the most appropriate schedule adjustments.

For all projects, however, time estimates are still largely subjective in nature, and depend both on the vagaries of the humans who produce these estimates and on the environment within which they operate. Some people are inclined to be more cautious (or should we say pessimistic, conserva-

---

[5]Hence the term GIGO commonly cited by PERT users: "Garbage In, Garbage Out."

tive or realistic?) than others and tend toward more generous time estimates. The system of rewards within which contractors operate might also influence their estimates for bidding purposes. Cost-plus contracts might well lead to underestimated times to enhance the probability of receiving the contract, while incentive-type contracts might lead to the opposite bias.

All these factors are of obvious concern to the manager who must make decisions based on activity time estimates supplied to him. King and others[6] have suggested that project managers establish a "super network" in addition to the basic network and time estimates which are openly displayed for all to see. The super network is the manager's private guide and incorporates *adjusted* time estimates based upon the manager's knowledge of past experience and the behavior of estimators. If reasonable adjustments can be made, the modified network would represent a more realistic and effective guide for planning and control purposes. Initial research efforts at developing adjustment models seem promising, but there is much to learn about estimating behavior before such models may be considered useful and reliable tools for project managers.

4. Already discussed in Chapter 4 are the assumptions of the probabilistic PERT model: *Activity duration is assumed to follow the Beta distribution; the standard deviation of the distribution is assumed to be one-sixth of its range; the mean is approximated by $\frac{1}{6}(t_o + 4t_m + t_p)$; and the variance in length of a project is assumed to be equal to the sum of the variances of activities on the critical path.* The theoretical problems of these assumptions are thoroughly examined by MacCrimmon and Ryavec in an article cited earlier.[7] In practice, apparently, the errors due to faulty assumptions and not-so-rigorous statistics are small compared to the errors in time estimates themselves.[8] PERT was developed for, and has generally been applied to, research and development types of projects with all their attendant uncertainties. Errors in time estimates of 10 or 20 per cent are common, and actual times which are twice the original estimates are not unknown. Given this

---

[6]See W. R. King and T. A. Wilson, "Subjective Time Estimates in Critical Path Analysis," *Mgt. Science*, **13**, No. 5 (Jan. 1967), 307–320; and W. R. King, D. M. Wittevrongel, and K. D. Hezel, "On the Analysis of Critical Path Time Estimating Behavior," *Mgt. Science*, **14**, No. 1 (Sept., 1967), 79–84. One interesting result of their studies was that, for the projects studied, the accuracy of time estimates did not improve over a period of time, that is, ". . . no significant changes in accuracy were observed either for preactivity estimates (as the beginning of the activity approached) or for estimates of the remaining duration of an activity (as the proportion of the activity remaining became smaller)." (From page 80 of the latter article.) This would seem to somewhat simplify the development of adjustment models, as the time element might be ignored.

[7]See page 49.

[8]MacCrimmon and Ryavec concluded that the PERT assumptions could lead to absolute errors in t_e and s_e on the order of 30 and 15 per cent, respectively, in rather extreme cases. In more reasonable situations, these errors would likely be reduced to 5 or 10 per cent, which, as they observe, are small compared to the likely errors in time estimates.

setting, most statistical problems associated with the PERT assumptions become irrelevant in a practical sense. Time estimates are the major source of error by a large margin.

Possible problems associated with the PERT procedure of picking a single critical path and calculating the expected length and variance of the project based on this path alone are solvable, as we noted in Chapter 4, if one is willing to apply the simulation techniques suggested by Van Slyke and Klingel (cited in that chapter). Admittedly the approach may be impractical in terms of computer capacity for very large, detailed projects. But if applied to smaller or aggregated networks, simulation could supply the manager with very useful statistical information concerning the major phases of his project. And, if desired, the method could be used on individual subsystems of the project to yield similar information for more detailed activities in the network. The cost of such studies could well be small compared to costs stemming from serious errors of judgment as a result of PERT's biased estimates of completion time distributions.

Associated with the uncertainties of activity durations has been the difficulty of even obtaining three time estimates per activity, as required by the PERT model. Project managers who request such estimates have often been told, "It is difficult enough to give *one* time estimate for an activity we've never done before, let alone *three*. The extreme values are especially problematical. What do you mean, for example, by 'pessimistic time'? If *everything* went wrong, we might never finish the activity. How pessimistic are we supposed to be in coming up with a pessimistic time?" Answers to questions like these are difficult to give. Guide lines are necessarily vague. It is not surprising that engineers, project leaders, foremen, or others who supply the estimates often come up with rather arbitrary values, as evidenced by the large number of estimates like 2–4–6 or 50–60–70. Such figures, of course, are of little value, and network calculations based on them tend to give an impression of greater precision than is justified.

As a result many, perhaps most, users of PERT have ceased using three time estimates per activity and require estimators to give only one figure—supposedly the best guess or expected duration for each activity. To be sure, there are other reasons for this practice. The sheer logistics of data handling for large projects with thousands of activities led to a desire for simplification in the model. And then, too, many managers untrained in statistical methods did not understand the meaning of expected value or "standard deviation of project length." There seemed to be little point in generating data which would be neither understood nor used.

In many ways this is regrettable. PERT represents an earnest, if not completely rigorous, attempt to cope with uncertainties in project management by some simple, rather straightforward applications of statistical theory. Despite some minor conceptual difficulties, it represents a step forward in dealing with a particular complex problem, and is certainly an improvement over models which deal with the problem deterministically— as if there were no uncertainties involved. In recent years, especially, managers have shown an appreciation for, and increasing understanding of, quantitative tools of decision making. Even though a knowledge of statistical methods as a whole requires a good deal more training than most managers have had, still the basic notions used in PERT are not beyond their ability to comprehend. It is unfortunate that the statistical elements of the PERT model were apparently tossed out before they could be proved—or improved—in the practice of project management.

5. The CPM model also has its special assumptions; one is, *The duration of an activity is linearly (and inversely) related to the cost of resources applied to the activity.* The assumption is a plausible one, and even if the linearity part of it is inaccurate, extensions of the CPM model allow for other functional relationships to be handled, as we indicated in Chapter 5. The problem with the cost-optimizing CPM model is not conceptual, however, but practical. Cost-time trade-off relationships are difficult to obtain in many instances, either because data are not available or because estimates are too bothersome or expensive to compile. The problem is similar to that described above for PERT: When asked for trade-off curves for each activity, engineers or foremen (or whoever supplies the information) frequently give somewhat arbitrary estimates, usually because they don't *know* what the actual relationships are. As a result most applications of CPM to date have been without the cost-optimizing feature. Thus CPM and PERT, in practical application, have tended to lose their distinctive features and to become essentially the same model.

While it is true that there is much of value in CPM to the manager aside from the cost-optimizing feature, we can still argue, as we did for PERT, that de-emphasis of its distinctive feature is unfortunate. Even if accurate cost-time data are not available, best guesses, unless completely arbitrary, are useful information and should help a project manager to arrive at better decisions on the average than no guesses at all. Most often those closely associated with a project or with particular activities will have some feeling for the nature of work that must be completed and can give at least a rough estimate of how much an activity could be expedited with certain additional resources. Even two points on a cost-time trade-off curve can supply the basic information needed for the optimizing calculations. Additional information, such as nonlinearities or discontinuities in the function, is useful, of course, and should help to yield more realistic results. Rough but reasonable estimates can be used to supply the project manager with a general idea of the cost-time trade-off relationships for the project as a whole —information which is certainly valuable to him. On the other hand, if only single time estimates are given for each activity, then the manager has no way of knowing if a schedule exists with costs lower than the one based on normal activity times. While the difficulty of obtaining the required data should be recognized, so should the potential benefits of using that data in the CPM model.

Need for Top Management Support

In a chapter commenting on the usefulness of network planning techniques, it is appropriate for us to note that the success or failure in applications of CPM and PERT depends to a large degree on the measure of support they receive from top management, particularly in large firms. There are several reasons why this support is cruical. First of all, CPM/PERT represents a new approach to project planning and scheduling, and there is bound to be resistance in any organization to major changes in old and comfortable ways of doing things. If a CPM/PERT system is initiated by top management or with their clear approval it has greater assurance of acceptance and success than if a lower-level agency attempts its installation. As we noted earlier, CPM and PERT techniques cut across organizational lines, not only in terms of activity identification, but also in managerial responsibilities. No one department is responsible for seeing that a project is kept on schedule. Activities on the critical path, or even a single critical activity, may involve several different departments. Thus, there is vital need for top level guidance and coordination. The system cannot be segmented and turned over to various parts of an organization for implementation. Nor can an existing agency of some department, like production control or operations research, be assigned responsibility for coordinating the whole system. A CPM/PERT group, if organized, should preferably report to top management rather than at some lower level within a subsection of the organization.

Top management consideration of expenses involved in a network is also needed. For a large project such expenses are not trivial; sometimes they run to several hundred thousand dollars. The Air Force has estimated that PERT costs have averaged between 0.1 and 0.5 per cent of total project costs, with the higher figure more typical of research and development programs. Expenditures of this magnitude merit top level analysis and control, especially during the start-up period of building a CPM/PERT capability.[9]

[9]Expected returns from such expenditures should be of even greater magnitude, and equally deserving of management's attention and analysis. Savings from network techniques—in better coordination, reduced delays, more accurate forecasts, fewer crash programs, and so on—are less easily identified than direct dollar costs and are often apparent only from the manager's projectwide viewpoint.

Also needed from top management is guidance concerning the standards of data collection and reporting. All agencies in an organization should supply data in a consistent form to facilitate processing, and output reports should be standardized in format and level of detail to facilitate their use not only within the firm but by customers or contractors. By their nature, CPM and PERT are capable of producing reams of various output reports. Management should specify the kinds of information and report summaries that would be most useful at various levels.

Decision Making at Various Levels of Management

The last mentioned item points out a fact which should be further amplified—that PERT and CPM are useful tools for management at various levels within an organization and at different times within the life cycle of a project. Further, ways in which the models are used and the information derived from them are dependent upon both the particular time-stage of the project and the organization level of a firm. For example, for maximum benefits network techniques should be applied during the early planning stages of a program. Many users of PERT and CPM have observed that primary benefits from using the techniques came in that stage, mostly because networking forced the integration of project planning. Planners are required to specify not only all the activities necessary to complete a project but also their technological dependencies. Network calculations then lay out clearly the implications of these interdependencies and aid the planners in finding problems that might otherwise be overlooked in large, complex projects. For example, one defense manufacturer found, as a result of using networks, that a prior plan required two missiles to be erected and launched on the same platform on the same day. And many examples of this nature may be cited.

At the planning level of project management, networks are usually constructed at an aggregate, nondetailed level, mainly to allow top management to study the feasibility and general outlines of a proposed project. When broad approval for a project has been given, these networks can be drawn with greater detail and more precision for purposes of scheduling and control.[10] Time scheduling of activities and resources follows from such networks, and they allow department or group managers to measure sub-

---

[10]The size of a project may affect the usefulness of CPM/PERT for scheduling purposes. After trying unsuccessfully to use PERT for scheduling the Dyna-Soar Program, Boeing Company concluded that the technique could not be used for detailed scheduling of large programs. Computer technology has advanced considerably since that time, however, and present computers and programs are capable of handling much larger networks. The logistics of handling networks with tens of thousands of activities still present problems of data gathering and information processing, however.

sequent progress against plans and to take appropriate action when needed. Further down the organizational ladder, the network graph is useful to foremen and others at the operating level in helping them to understand the sequencing of jobs and the necessity of pushing those that are critical. They can more readily see the relationships of activities for which they are responsible and predecessor or successor activities which fall in other areas or departments.

Conclusion

For large, nonrepetitive operations or projects CPM, PERT, and related network techniques are useful aids, indeed, for project managers. As a summary to our exposition of CPM and PERT, we note some of their features and characteristics that make them powerful and flexible tools for decision making:

1. As discussed immediately above, they are useful at several stages of project management—from the early planning stages, when various alternative programs or procedures are being considered; to the scheduling phase, when time and resource schedules are laid out; and finally in the operational phase, when used as a control device to measure actual versus planned progress.
2. They are straightforward in concept and easily explainable to the layman with no background in network theory. Data calculations, while tedious for large projects, are not difficult. Basic critical path data may be hand calculated with reasonable speed for projects with up to 500 or 600 activities. Computer programs are readily available for larger projects.
3. The network graph displays in a simple and direct way the complex interrelations of activities which comprise a project. Managers of various subdivisions of the project may quickly perceive from the graph how their portion affects, and is affected by, other parts of the project.
4. Network calculations pinpoint attention to the relatively small subset of activities in a project which are critical to its completion. Managerial action is thus focused on exceptional problems, contributing to more reliable planning and more effective control.
5. CPM enables the manager to reasonably estimate total project costs for various completion dates. These various trade-off possibilities, along with other decision criteria, enable him to select an optimum or near-optimum schedule.
6. CPM and PERT are applicable to many types of projects—from aerospace development projects to large construction and maintenance jobs, from new product introduction programs to missile countdown procedures. Moreover, they may be applied at several levels within a given project, from a single department working on a subsystem to multi-plant operations within a large corporation.
7. As simulation tools, they enable the manager to project into the

future the effects of planned or unanticipated changes and to take appropriate action when such projections indicate the need for it. Thus, for example, the manager can quickly study the effects of crash programs and can anticipate in advance potential resource bottlenecks that might result from shortening certain critical jobs.

When wisely used by a project manager who understands their strengths and limitations, CPM and PERT can be effective amplifiers of his managerial skills.

Bibliography

The following bibliography on network planning and scheduling techniques is drawn from a large and growing body of literature on the subject. We have sought to create a representative rather than a comprehensive list. Additionally, we have attempted to make the list somewhat more useful to the reader by categorizing the entries according to general content or purpose. Some explanation of the subheadings is in order.

First listed are general sources, mostly of an expository nature, whose major purpose is to acquaint the reader with the basic network techniques. Most of these are articles which have appeared in a wide variety of journals and magazines. We have attempted to select explanatory rather than descriptive articles, omitting, for the most part, short news articles of from one to four pages from newspapers and trade journals. Following the articles is a list of books primarily devoted to project management and network analysis. Some of these are "how-to-do-it" books (for example, those by Miller, The Federal Electric Corporation, and Martino), while others contain material of theoretical interest (those by Battersby, Kelley, and Moder and Phillips).

The next major heading is "Theory: Analyses and Extensions of Network Scheduling Techniques," followed by a number of subtopics. Entries in this section are drawn mainly from technical journals and were typically authored by persons more interested in theoretical rather than practical aspects of the techniques. Their purpose has been to analyze critically rather than to describe the models and to suggest modifications or extensions of conceptual interest. The subheadings reflect what we feel have been some of the major areas of analysis and research. Not all articles fit neatly into our categories, however, and some of our placement decisions may seem a little arbitrary. Fulkerson's article, "A Network Flow Computation for Project Cost Curves," for example, obviously straddles our categories, "Cost-Time-Performance Relationships" and "Network Flow Interpretation," although we placed it in the latter.

The final section, "Managerial and Operational Aspects," lists articles with a more practical slant—those describing particular applications of PERT and CPM or evaluating such applications from a managerial viewpoint. Operational rather than theoretical strengths and weaknesses of the models are stressed. The section closes with a list of bibliographical sources which will guide the interested reader to more articles—and perhaps more bibliographies!

A. General

Original Descriptions

Kelley, James E., Jr., and Morgan R. Walker, "Critical Path Planning and Scheduling," *Proceedings of the Eastern Joint Computer Conference*, Boston, Mass. (1959), pp. 160–173.

PERT, Program Evaluation Research Task, Phase I Summary Report, Special Projects Office, Bureau of Ordinance, 7, Department of the Navy, Washington, D. C. (July, 1958), pp. 646–669.

Expository Articles

Archibald, R. D., "PERT and the Role of the Computer," *Computers and Automation*, 12, 7 (July, 1963), pp. 26–30.

Battersby, A., "Network Flow Analysis," *The Accountant*, 147, 4574 (1962), pp. 184–186; and 147, 4575 (1962), pp. 228–231.

Burgher, P. H., "PERT and the Auditor," *The Accounting Review*, 39 (1964), pp. 103–120.

Fazar, W., "Navy's PERT System," *Federal Accountant*, 11 (December, 1961), pp. 123–136.

———, "The Origin of PERT," *The Controller*, (December, 1962), pp. 598–602, 618–621.

Levy, F. K., G. L. Thompson, and J. D. Wiest, "The ABC's of the Critical Path Method," *Harvard Business Review*, 41, 5 (September-October, 1963), pp. 98–108.

Malcolm, Donald G., John H. Roseboom, Charles E. Clark, and Willard Fazar, "Applications of a Technique for Research and Development Program Evaluation," *Opns. Res.*, 7, 5 (September-October, 1959), pp. 646–669.

———, "PERT: A Designed Management Information System," *Industrial Management*, 3 (June, 1961), pp. 23–32.

———, "PERT: An Automated R[esearch] and D[evelopment] Management

Information System," *Proc. 12th Annual National American Institute of Industrial Engineers Conference* (1961), pp. 77–89.

Martino, R., "New Way to Analyze and Plan Operations and Projects Will Save You Time and Cash," *Oil/Gas World*, 3 (September, 1959), pp. 38–46.

Miller, R. W., "How to Plan and Control with PERT," *Harvard Business Review*, 40, 2 (March-April, 1962), pp. 93–104.

Norden, P., "On the Anatomy of Development Projects," *IRE Trans. Eng. Mgt.*, 7, 1 (March, 1960), pp. 34–42.

Paige, H. W., "How PERT-Cost Helps the General Manager," *Harvard Business Review*, 41, 6 (November-December, 1963), pp. 87–95.

Roper, Don E., "Critical Path Scheduling," *J. Indust. Eng.* XV, 2 (March-April, 1964).

Sobczak, T. U., "A Look at Network Planning," *IRE Trans. Eng. Mgt.*, 9, 3 (September, 1962), pp. 113–116.

Usry, M. F., "PERT/Cost and the Capital Expenditure Control Program," *J. Accountancy*, 115, 3 (March, 1963), pp. 83–86.

Expository Books

Battersby, A., *Network Analysis for Planning and Scheduling.* London: Macmillan & Company, Ltd., 1967.

Federal Electric Corporation, *A Programmed Introduction to PERT.* New York: John Wiley & Sons, Inc., 1963.

Hajek, Victor G., *Project Engineering.* New York: McGraw-Hill Book Company, 1965.

Hansen, B. J., *Practical PERT.* Washington, D. C.: American Aviation Publication, 1964.

Kelley, J. E., Jr., *Critical Path Scheduling*, Vol. 11 of the SIAM Series in Applied Mathematics. New York: John Wiley & Sons, Inc. (forthcoming).

Learning Systems Italiana, Spa., *PERT, Program Evaluation and Review Technique.* Rome: Edizione Centro Europeo Coordinamento Istruzione Lavoro, 1965.

Martino, R. L., *Finding the Critical Path.* New York: American Management Association, 1964.

———, *Applied Operational Planning.* Project Management and Control Series, Vol. II, New York: American Management Association, 1964.

Miller, R. W., *Schedule, Cost and Profit Control with PERT.* New York: McGraw-Hill Book Company, 1963.

Moder, J. J. and C. R. Phillips, *Project Management with CPM and PERT.* New York: Reinhold Publishing Corp., 1964.

Muth, J. F. and G. L. Thompson (eds.), *Industrial Scheduling.* Englewood Cliffs, N. J.: Prentice-Hall, Inc., 1963.

O'Brien, J. J., *CPM in Construction Management.* New York: McGraw-Hill Book Company, 1965.

Secretary of Defense and National Aeronautics and Space Administration, *DOD and NASA Guide, PERT Cost Systems Design.* Washington, D. C.: Government Printing Office, June 1962.

Shaffer, L. R., J. B. Ritter, and W. L. Meyer, *Critical Path Method.* New York: McGraw-Hill Book Company, 1965.

USAF PERT-TIME System Description Manual, Vol. 1, September, 1963.

B. Theory : Analyses and Extensions of Network Scheduling Techniques

Statistical Considerations and Problems

Charnes, A., W. W. Cooper, and G. L. Thompson, "Critical Path Analysis Via Chance Constrained and Stochastic Programming," *Opns. Res.*, 12, 3 (May-June, 1964), pp. 460–470.

Clark, C. E., "The PERT Model for the Distribution of an Activity Time," *Opns. Res.*, 10, 3 (May-June, 1962), pp. 405–406.

Clingen, C. T., "A Modification of Fulkerson's PERT Algorithm," *Opns. Res.*, 12, 4 (July-August, 1964), pp. 629–632.

Donaldson, W. A., "The Estimation of the Mean and Variance of a 'PERT' Activity Time," *Opns. Res.*, 13, 3 (May-June, 1965), pp. 382–385 and "Note" by H. Coon, pp. 386–387.

Fulkerson, D. R, "Expected Critical Path Lengths in PERT Networks," *Opns. Res.*, 10, 6 (November-December, 1962), pp. 808–817.

Grubbs, F. E., "Attempts to Validate Certain PERT Statistics or 'Picking on PERT'," *Opns. Res.*, 10, 6 (November-December, 1962), pp. 912–915.

———, "Corrigenda," *Opns. Res.*, 11, 1 (January-February, 1963), p. 156.

Healy, T., "Activity Subdivision and PERT Probability Statements," *Opns. Res.*, 9, 3 (May-June, 1961), pp. 341–348. Comments by C. Clark, *Opns. Res.*, 9, 3 (May-June, 1961), p. 348. Comments by H. Millstein, *Opns. Res.*, 9, 3 (May-June, 1961), p. 349. Comments by J. Roseboom, *Opns. Res.*, 9, 6 (November-December, 1961), p. 909.

Jewell, W. S., "Risk-Taking in Critical Path Analysis," *Mgt. Science*, 11, 3 (January, 1965), pp. 438–443.

King, W. R., and T. A. Wilson, "Subjective Time Estimates in Critical Path Analysis," *Mgt. Science*, 13, 5 (January, 1967), pp. 307–320.

———, D. M. Wittevrongel, and K. D. Hezel, "On the Analysis of Critical Path Time Estimating Behavior," *Mgt. Science*, 14, 1 (September, 1967), pp. 79–84.

Klingel, A. R., Jr., "Bias in PERT Project Completion Time Calculations for a Real Network," *Mgt. Science*, 13, 4 (December, 1966), pp. B-194 to B-201.

Lùkaszewicz, J., "On the Estimation of Errors Introduced by Standard Assumptions Concerning the Distribution of Activity Duration in PERT Calculations," *Opns. Res.*, 13, 2 (March-April, 1965), pp. 326–327.

MacCrimmon, K. R. and C. A. Ryavec, "An Analytical Study of the PERT Assumptions," *Opns. Res.*, 12, 1 (January-February, 1964), pp. 16–37.

Van Slyke, R. M., "Monte Carlo Methods and the PERT Problem," *Opns. Res.*, 11, 5 (September-October, 1963), pp. 839–860.

Welsh, D. J. A., "Errors Introduced by a PERT Assumption," *Opns. Res.*, 13, 1 (January-February, 1965), pp. 141–143.

Cost-Time-Performance Relationships

Berman, E. B., "Resource Allocation in a PERT Network under Continuous Activity Time-Cost Functions," *Mgt. Science*, 10, 4 (July, 1964), pp. 734–745.

Bildson, R. A. and J. R. Gillespie, "Critical Path Planning—PERT Integration," *Opns. Res.*, 10, 6 (November-December, 1962), pp. 909–912.

Burgess, A. R. and J. B. Killebrew, "Variation in Activity Level on a Cyclical Arrow Diagram," *J. Indust. Eng.*, XIII (March-April, 1962), pp. 76–83.

Clark, C., "The Optimum Allocation of Resources Among the Activities of a Network," *J. Indust. Eng.*, XII (January-February, 1961), pp. 11–17.

Kelley, J., "Critical-Path Planning and Scheduling: Mathematical Basis," *Opns. Res.*, 9, 3 (May-June, 1961), pp. 296–320.

Malcolm, D. G., "Reliability Maturity Index (RMI)—An Extension of PERT into Reliability Management," *J. Indust. Eng.*, XIV (January-February, 1963), pp. 3-12.

McGee, A. A. and M. D. Markarian, "Optimum Allocation of Research/Engineering Manpower within a Multi-Project Organizational Structure," *IRE Trans. Eng. Mgt.*, 9 (1962), pp. 104–108.

Meyer, W. L. and L. R. Shaffer, "Extensions of the Critical Path Method Through the Application of Integer Programming," Department of Civil Engineering, University of Illinois (July, 1963).

Network Flow Interpretation

Charnes, A. and W. W. Cooper, "A Network Interpretation and a Directed Subdual Algorithm for Critical Path Scheduling," *J. Indust. Eng.*, XIII, 4 (July-August, 1962), pp. 213–219.

Fulkerson, D., "A Network Flow Computation for Project Cost Curves," *Mgt. Science*, 7, 2 (January, 1961), pp. 167–178.

———, "Scheduling in Project Networks," The RAND Corporation, RM-4137-PR (June, 1964).

Ivanescu, P. L., "Some Network Flow Problems Solved with Pseudo-Boolean Programming," *Opns. Res.*, 13, 3 (May-June, 1965), pp. 388–399.

Precedence Relationships; Network Decomposition

Jewell, W. S., "Divisible Activities in Critical Path Analysis," *Opns. Res.*, 13, 5 (September-October, 1965), pp. 747–760.

Parikh, S. C. and W. S. Jewell, "Decomposition of Project Networks," *Mgt. Science*, 11, 3 (January, 1965), pp. 444–459; and "Note" by R. W. Blanning and A. G. Rao, 12, 1 (September, 1965), pp. 145–148.

Probabilistic and Decision Networks

Crowston, W. and G. L. Thompson, "Decision CPM: A Method for Simultaneous Planning, Scheduling and Control of Projects," *Opns. Res.*, 15, 3 (May-June, 1967), pp. 407–426.

Eisner, H., "A Generalized Network Approach to the Planning and Scheduling of a Research Project," *Opns. Res.*, 10, 1 (January-February, 1962), pp. 115–125.

Elmaghraby, S. E., "An Algebra for the Analysis of Generalized Activity Networks," *Mgt. Science*, 10, 3 (April, 1964), pp. 494–514.

Freeman, R., "A Generalized Network Approach to Project Activity Sequencing," *IRE Trans. Eng. Mgt.*, 7, 3 (September, 1960), pp. 103–107.

Pritsker, A. A. B. and W. W. Rapp, "GERT: Graphical Evaluation and Review Technique, Part I: Fundamentals," *J. Indust. Eng.*, XVII, 5 (May, 1966). Part II: "Probabilistic and Industrial Engineering Applications," XVII, 6 (June, 1966).

Programming

Goldberg, C. R., "An Algorithm for the Sequential Solution of Schedule Networks," *Opns. Res.*, 12, 3 (May-June, 1964), pp. 499–502.

Kahn, A. B., "Skeletal Structure of PERT and CPA Computer Programs," *Communic. of ACM*, 6, 8 (August, 1963), pp. 473–479.

———, "Topological Sorting of Large Network," *Communic. of ACM*, 5, 11 (November, 1962), pp. 558–562.

Lass, S. E., "PERT Time Calculations Without Topological Ordering," *Communic. of ACM*, 8, 3 (March, 1965), pp. 172–174.

Lasser, D., "Topological Ordering of a List of Randomly-Numbered Elements of a Network," *Communic. of ACM*, 4, 4 (April, 1961), pp. 167–168.

Matozzi, M., "How to do CPM Scheduling Without an Arrow Diagram," *Eng. News-Record*, 170 (May 9, 1963), pp. 30–31.

Matye, T. and G. Rich, "PERT/PEP Planning and Programming on [Electric Accounting Machines]," *J. Machine Accounting*, 12 (July, 1961), pp. 6–13.

Moder, J. J., "How to Do CPM Scheduling Without a Computer," *Eng. News-Record*, 170 (March 14, 1963), pp. 30–36.

Montalbano, M., "High Speed Calculation of the Critical Paths of Large Networks," *IBM Systems Journal*, 6, 3 (1967), pp. 163–191.

Phillips, C. R., "Fifteen Key Features of Computer Programs for CPM and PERT," *J. Indust. Eng.*, XV (January-February, 1964), pp. 14–20.

Prostick, J., "Loop Tracing in PEP/PERT Networks," (abstract), *Communic. of ACM*, 4, 7 (July, 1961), p. 304.

Solomon, N. B., "Automated Methods in PERT Processing," *Computers and Automation*, 14, 1 (January, 1965), pp. 18-22.

Resource Allocation to Project Networks

Alpert, R. and D. S. Orkand, "A Time-Resource Trade-off Model for Aiding Management Decisions," Technical Paper No. 12, Operations Research, Inc., Silver Spring, Md. (1962).

Blair, R. J., "Critical Path Resources Simulation and Scheduling," *IRE Trans. Eng. Mgt.* 10, 3 (September, 1963), pp. 100–103.

Davis, E. W., "Resource Allocation in Project Network Models—A Survey," *J. Indust. Eng.*, XVII, 4 (April, 1966), pp. 177–188.

De Ambrogio, W., "A Computer Program for Multiproject Scheduling with Smoothing of Resource Requirements," Paper, Institute of Management Sciences Conference, Zurich (September, 1964).

De Witte, L., "Manpower Leveling of PERT Networks," *Data Processing for Science/Engineering*, 2, 2 (1964), p. 29.

Ghare, P. M. "Optimal Resource Allocation in Activity Networks," Paper, Operations Research Society of America Meeting, Houston, Texas (November, 1965).

Hooper, P. C., "Resource Allocation and Levelling," Proceedings of the Third CPA Symposium, Operational Research Society, London (1965).

Kelley, James E., Jr., "The Critical Path Method: Resources Planning and Scheduling," Chapt. 21 in *Industrial Scheduling*, eds. J. F. Math and G. L. Thompson. Englewood Cliffs, N. J.: Prentice-Hall, Inc., 1963.

Lambourn, S., "Resource Allocation and Multiproject Scheduling (RAMPS), A New Tool in Planning and Control," *Computer Journal*, 5, 4 (January, 1963), pp. 300–304.

Levy, F. K., G. L. Thompson, and J. D. Wiest, "Multi-Ship, Multi-Shop, Workload Smoothing Program," *Naval Research Logistics Quarterly*, 9, 1 (March, 1962), pp. 37–44.

Martino, R. L., *Resource Allocation and Scheduling*, Project Management and Control Series, Vol. III. New York: American Management Association, 1965.

Mize, J. H., "A Heuristic Scheduling Model for Multi-Project Organizations." Ph. D. thesis, Purdue University, August, 1964.

Moshman, J., J. Johnson and Madalyn Larsen, "RAMPS: A Technique for Resource Allocation and Multiproject Scheduling," Proceedings of the 1963 Spring Joint Computer Conference.

Pascoe, T. L., "An Experimental Comparison of Heuristic Methods for Allocating Resources," Ph. D. thesis, Engineering Dept., Cambridge University, 1965.

RAMPS Training Text, CEIR Inc., Arlington, Va., 1962.

RAMPS Users Guide, CEIR Inc., Arlington, Va., 1962.

Wiest, J. D., "The Scheduling of Large Projects with Limited Resources." Ph. D. thesis, Carnegie Institute of Technology, 1963.

———, "Some Properties of Schedules for Large Projects with Limited Resources," *Opns. Res.*, 12, 3 (May-June, 1964), pp. 395–418.

———, "A Heuristic Model for Scheduling Large Projects with Limited Resources," *Mgt. Science*, 13, 6 (February, 1967), pp. B359–B377.

Wilson, R. C., "Assembly Line Balancing and Resource Scheduling," University of Michigan Summer Conference on Production and Inventory Control, 1964.

C. Managerial and Operational Aspects

Applications

Beutel, M. L., "Computer Estimates Costs, Saves Time, Money," *Eng. News-Record*, 170 (February 28, 1963), pp. 26–30.

Butler, R. A., "Systems Design with PERT," *J. Data Management*, 3, 6 (June, 1965), pp. 22–25.

Childs, M. R., "Does PERT Work for Small Projects?" *Data Processing*, 4 (1962), pp. 32–35.

Fazar, W., "Advanced Management Systems for Advanced Weapon Systems," *Conf. Proc. 5th Nat. Convn. on Military Electronics* (1961), 32–43.

———, "Progress Reporting in the Special Projects Office," *Navy Mgmt. Review*, 4 (April, 1959), pp. 9–15.

Glasser, L. and R. Young, "Critical Path Planning, and Scheduling: Application to Engineering and Construction," *Chem. Eng. Progress*, 57 (November, 1961), pp. 60–65.

Gorham, W., "An Application of a Network Flow Model to Personnel Planning," *IRE Trans. Eng. Mgt.*, 10, 3 (September, 1963), pp. 113–123.

Hallbauer, R. M., "CPM Facilitates Project Planning and Cost Control," *Cost and Management*, 39, 4 (April, 1965), pp. 167–175.

Kelley, J., "Critical-Path Planning and Scheduling: Case Histories," (abstract), *Opns. Res.*, 8 (1960), B109.

Kurzeja, J. T., "When Work Schedules Need Computers," *Hydrocarbon Process. and Petrol. Refiner*, 44, 4 (April, 1965), pp. 171–174.

Mark, E. J., "How Critical Path Method Controls Piping Installation Progress," *Heating, Piping, and Air Condit.*, 9 (September, 1963), pp. 121–126.

Newnham, D. E., *et al.*, "A PERT Control Center for Management of Major Ballistic Missile Modifications Programs," *J. Indus. Eng.* XVI, 4 (July-August, 1965).

Odom, Ralph G. and E. Blystone, "A Case Study of CPM in a Manufacturing Situation," *J. Indust. Eng.*, XV, 6 (November-December, 1964).

Pearlman, J., "Engineering Program Planning and Control Through the Use of PERT," *IRE Trans. Eng. Mgt.*, 7, 12 (December, 1960), pp. 125–134.

Peterson, R. J., "CPM Helps an A-E Consultant Schedule Manpower," *Eng. News-Record*, 170 (June 27, 1963), pp. 22–25.

Reeves, E., "Critical Path Speeds Refinery Revamp," *Canadian Chem. Processing*, 44 (October, 1960), pp. 74–76.

Robinson, I. G., "4 Simple Steps—The PERT Approach to Plant Layout," *Factory* (September, 1965), pp. 104–105.

Vaughen, B. W. and G. V. Kedrowsky, "SYNCOM Event Schedule Networks— The Best of PERT," *IRE Trans. Eng. Mgt.*, 10, 3 (September, 1963), pp. 104–112.

Wong, Y., "Critical Path Analysis for New Product Planning," *J. Marketing*, 28, 4 (October, 1964), pp. 53–59.

Evaluations and Critiques

Avots, I., "The Management Side of PERT," *California Mgt. Review*, 4, 2 (Winter, 1962), pp. 16–27.

Barmby, J. G., "The Applicability of PERT as a Management Tool," *IRE Trans. Eng. Mgt.*, 9, 3 (September, 1962), pp. 130–131.

Boulanger, D., "Program Evaluation and Review Technique (PERT): A Case Study Application With Analysis," *Advanced Mgmt.*, 26 (July-August, 1961), pp. 7–12.

Boverie, R. T., "The Practicalities of PERT," *IRE Trans. Eng. Mgt.*, 10, 1 (March, 1963), pp. 3–5.

Dooley, A., "Interpretations of PERT," *Harvard Business Review*, 42, 6 (November-December, 1964), pp. 160–168.

Eyring, Henry B., "Evaluation of Planning Models for Research and Development Projects," D.B.A. thesis, Harvard University, June, 1963.

———, "Some Sources of Uncertainty in Engineering Design Projects," The RAND Corporation, RM-4503 (September, 1965).

Frambes, R., "Next Big Step for PERT," *Aerospace Mgmt.*, 4 (October, 1961), pp. 77–78.

Fry, B. L., "SCANS—System Description and Comparison with PERT," *IRE Trans. Eng. Mgt.*, 9, 3 (September, 1962), pp. 122–129.

Geddes, P., "How Good is PERT?" *Aerospace Mgmt.*, 4 (September, 1961), pp. 41–43.

Gleason, W. J., Jr., and J. J. Ranieri, "First Five Years of the Critical-Path Method," *J. Construct. Division, Proc. Am. Soc. Civil Engin.*, 90, C01, Proceeding Paper No. 3892 (March, 1964), pp. 27–36.

Hawthorne, R., "PERT and PEP: Useful Tools or Timewasters?" *Space/Aeronautics*, 36 (August, 1961), pp. 56–58.

Hill, L. S., "Communications, Semantics, and Information Systems," *J. Indust. Eng.*, XVI, 2 (March-April, 1965), pp. 131–135.

———, "Perspective: Some Possible Pitfalls in the Design and Use of PERT Networking," *J. Acad. Management*, 8, 2 (June, 1965), pp. 139–145.

———, "Management Planning and Control of Research and Technology Projects," The RAND Corporation, RM-4921-PR (June 1966).

———, "Some Cost Accounting Problems in PERT Cost," *J. Indust. Eng.*, XVII, 2 (February, 1966), pp. 87–91.

Mintz, S. and J. Taul, "Towards a Simplified Decision Making Criteria for PERT-Type Systems: The [Value Index Predictor] Index" (abstract), *Opns. Res.*, 9 (1961), B130.

Murray, J. E., "Consideration of PERT Assumptions," *IRE Trans. Eng. Mgt.* 10, 3 (September, 1963), pp. 94–99.

Paige, Millard W., "How PERT-COST Helps the General Manager," *Harvard Business Review*, 41, 6 (November-December, 1963), pp. 87–95.

Pocock, J. W., "PERT as an Analytical Aid for Program Planning—Its Payoff and Problems," *Opns. Res.*, 10, 6 (November-December, 1962), pp. 893–903.

Roman, D. D., "The PERT Systems: An Appraisal of Program Evaluation Review Technique," *J. Acad. Management*, 5, 1 (April, 1962), pp. 57–65.

Schoderbek, P. P., "A Study of the Applications of PERT," *J. Acad. Management*, 8, 3 (September, 1965), pp. 199–210.

Simon, C., "Standardization: The Key to Making PERT Work," (abstract), *Opns. Res.*, 9 (1961), B140.

Thompson, R. E., "PERT—Tool for R and D Project Decision Making," *IRE Trans. Eng. Mgt.*, 9, 3 (September, 1962), pp. 116–121.

Thompson, V., "PERT: Pro and Con About This Technique," *Data Processing*, 3 (October, 1961), pp. 40–44.

Bibliographies on Network Techniques

Bigelow, C. G., "Bibliography on Project Planning and Control by Network Analysis: 1959–1961," *Opns. Res.*, 10, 5 (September-October, 1962), pp. 729–732.

Dooley, A. R., "Interpretations of PERT," *Harvard Business Review*, 42, 2 (March-April, 1964), pp. 160–162.

Fry, B. L., "Selected References on PERT and Related Topics," *IRE Trans. Eng. Mgt.*, 10, 3 (September, 1963), pp. 150–151.

Lerda-Olberg, S., "Bibliography on Network-Based Project Planning and Control Techniques: 1962–1965," *Opns. Res.*, 14, 5 (September-October, 1966), pp. 925–931..

U. S. Air Force, PERT Orientation Center, *Bibliography: PERT and Other Management Systems and Techniques*, Washington, D. C., June, 1963.

Exercises

To test your understanding of the concepts presented throughout this book, you may wish to work some or all of the problems printed below. They have been grouped according to chapter, with three or more problems drawn from Chapters 2, 3, 4, 5, and 7. Answers to the problems are given at the end of this section.

CHAPTER 2—Constructing Networks

1. As a college student, your project is College Education, with Graduation marking the end event.
   a. Draw a network representing the project. Include necessary courses with their precedence relationships (where course requirements are relevant), special examinations, projects, research, thesis writing, and so forth, required for the degree.
2. You are preparing to leave on an extended business or vacation trip.
   a. Set down in network form the jobs that must be done before you go.
3. You are planning to undertake one of the following projects: Remodel Kitchen, Add New Bedroom, or Move to New House.
   a. Draw the network of activities that you anticipate would be required.
4. The Wonder Widget is manufactured in six steps, labeled A through F. Because of its size and complexity, the Wonder Widget is produced one-at-a-time. Mr. Green, the production control manager, thinks that network scheduling techniques might be useful in planning future production. He asked the foreman in charge of Widgets about the six steps required in

production and the order in which the steps took place. He recorded the following information:

A is the first step and precedes B and C

C precedes D and E

B follows D and precedes E

F follows E

D is a successor of F

a. Draw an activity-on-node diagram for Mr. Green. Do you see any problems with the resulting network?

b. On checking with the foreman again, Mr. Green corrects his last note to read "D is a *predecessor* of F." Draw an arrow diagram for the revised project. How many dummy activities did you use in your network?

5. Presentation of a stage play involves a number of activities which precede the opening night "curtain-up" call. Thus, such a presentation may be regarded as a project and analyzed by network techniques. Listed below in random fashion is a collection of activities which must be completed before the first public performance. Others might be included, but assume that the list is essentially complete.

a. Draw a network for this project, indicating the precedence relationships which you feel are necessary. Quite likely there is no unique ordering of activities upon which all persons would agree; differences of opinion will exist. But decide on that ordering which seems most logical to you. Either an arrow or an activity-on-node diagram may be used.

Activities for Project On Stage

Design of scenery
Tryouts for actors
Selection of stage manager
Publicity—posters, mail advertisements
Selection of director
Initial rehearsals
Arrangements for hall
Selection of play
Selection of business manager
Final dress rehearsal
Constructing and painting scenery
Sale of tickets
Opening night performance
Publicity—newspaper story
Advanced rehearsals (with props)
Making or renting costumes
Obtaining props (set furnishings, items used by actors, etc.)
Erection of scenery

Chapter 3—Network Calculations

1. A small maintenance project consists of the following ten jobs, whose precedence relationships are identified by their node numbers:

Job Name	Alternate (initial node, final node)	Estimated Duration (days)
a	(1,2)	2
b	(2,3)	3
c	(2,4)	5
d	(3,5)	4
e	(3,6)	1
f	(4,6)	6
g	(4,7)	2
h	(5,8)	8
i	(6,8)	7
j	(7,8)	4

a. Draw an arrow diagram representing the project.
b. Calculate early and late occurrence times for each event (node).
c. How much slack does job (3, 5) have? Job (4, 6)? Job (7, 8)?
d. Which jobs are critical?
e. If job (2, 3) were to take six days instead of three, how would the project finish date be affected?
f. Do any jobs have free slack? If so, which ones and how much?

2. Each weekday morning Mr. Brady and his wife and children complete a set of activities which are necessary to start Mr. Brady on his way to the office. An analysis of the project Getting Mr. Brady to Work reveals the following list of relevant activities, their durations, and their predecessor relationships:

Activity	Description	Duration (minutes)	Immediate Predecessors
Performed by Mr. Brady			
1	Alarm goes off	0	—
2	Get up, shut off alarm, and turn up heat	2	1
3	Return to bed until house warms up	10	2
4	Get up, shave, and shower	22	3
5	Get dressed	10	4, 13
6	Eat breakfast	20	5, 15
7	Brush teeth	3	6, 20
8	Put on tie and coat	4	7
9	Pick up briefcase, hat, and lunch	2	8, 17
10	Kiss wife goodbye	1	9, 18

Activity	Description	Duration (minutes)	Immediate Predecessors
11	Walk to bus stop	4	10
12	Catch bus	0	11
Performed by Mrs. Brady			
13	Get up, iron shirt for husband	16	3
14	Wake up children	3	13
15	Prepare breakfast	20	14
16	Eat breakfast	20	15
17	Pack lunch	10	16
18	Comb hair, put on lipstick	3	7, 17
Performed by children			
19	Get up	5	14
20	Use bathroom	37	4, 19

a. Draw an arrow diagram complete with dummy activities for the project Getting Mr. Brady to Work.

b. Calculate early and late *node* occurrence times.

c. For each activity calculate early start and finish times, late start and finish times, total slack, and free slack, based on minimum completion time.

d. Mark the critical path and state its length.

e. How early must the alarm go off if Mr. Brady is to catch a 7:30 A.M. bus?

f. If Mr. Brady wanted to obtain more sleep by having the alarm go off later and still catch his bus, would it help for him to:
   1. Take less time showering?
   2. Eat faster?
   3. Have his shirts done at the laundry?
   4. Buy his lunch at work?
   5. Wait until he got to work to brush his teeth?
   6. Complain about the time his children take in the bathroom?

g. Is there any time when Mr. Brady could read the newspaper for a few minutes without delaying his arrival at the bus stop—without setting the alarm for an earlier time? Similarly, is there any time when Mrs. Brady could read the newspaper?

h. Draw an activity-on-node diagram for the project and mark the critical path. How does the number of precedence-relation arrows of this graph compare with the number of activity arrows, including those for dummy activities, of the diagram for (a)?

3. The major jobs to be completed in building a particular type of house are listed below, along with their necessary predecessors and estimated duration times:

Job	Description	Immediate Predecessors	Duration (days)
1	Start : obtain building permit	—	1
2	Clear lot and grade for slab	1	2
3	Place concrete forms, reinforcement rods, sewer lines	2	2
4	Pour slab	3	1
5	Erect wooden frame, including roof	4	5
6	Fasten exterior sheathing	5	2
7	Install rough plumbing	5	3
8	Install rough wiring	5	2
9	Insulate outside walls	6, 7, 8, 27	1
10	Sheetrock and plaster inside walls	9	3
11	Do rough carpentry, including window and door frames	5	5
12	Do finish carpentry : cabinets, trim moldings, paneling	10, 11	10
13	Sand, stain, and varnish wood paneling and cabinets	12	3
14	Lay Formica counter surfaces in kitchen	13	1
15	Install tubs and shower basins	10, 11	1
16	Lay bathroom tile	15	2
17	Install remaining plumbing fixtures	14, 16	1
18	Sand and paint interior walls and trim	17	5
19	Lay flooring (wood and vinyl)	18	2
20	Wallpaper selected surfaces	18	2
21	Install kitchen appliances	18	1
22	Install hot water heater	7	1
23	Install heating and cooling ducts	5	3
24	Install furnace and air conditioner	8, 23	1
25	Complete exterior trim	6	3
26	Lay brickwork (exterior walls plus inside fireplace)	25	5
27	Shingle roof	5	2
28	Attach gutters and downspouts	26, 27	2
29	Paint exterior trim	28	2
30	Place insulation in attic	10, 26	1
31	Grade, lay forms for walks and driveways	26	1
32	Pour walks and driveway	31	1
33	Finish grading	32, 37	1
34	Landscape yard	33	2
35	Install electrical outlets, switches, lighting fixtures	20, 21, 22, 24	1
36	Final hookup of electrical system	35	1
37	Clean up interior and exterior, including yard	19, 29, 30, 35	1
38	Lay carpeting	37	2
39	Attach cabinet fixtures	18	1
40	Finish : close out house	34, 36, 38, 39	1

a. Draw an activity-on-node diagram, labeling each node.
b. Draw an arrow diagram. Include necessary dummy jobs. Which representation do you prefer? Why?
c. Using either diagram, calculate early start and finish times, late start and finish times, and total slack for each job.

   d. Identify the critical path. What is the minimum length of the project?
   e. Which jobs may be delayed without delaying the early start time of any other job? State the amount of free slack of these jobs.
   f. If you were the contractor, how would you reduce the construction time by three days? By ten days?
   g. Do you foresee any problems of workmen interfering with each other's activities? (Assume an early start schedule.)

Chapter 4—PERT Problems

1. If the critical path of a project is 20 months long with a standard deviation of 4 months, what is the probability that the project will be completed within:
   a. 20 months?
   b. 18 months?
   c. 24 months?

2. PERT calculations yield a project length of 60 weeks, with variance of 9. Within how many weeks would you expect the project to be completed with probability 0.95? (That is, what is the project length that you would expect to be exceeded only 5 per cent of the time if the project were repeated many times in an identical manner?)

3. A father notes that when his teen-age daughter uses the telephone, she takes no less than five minutes for a call and sometimes as much as an hour. Fifteen-minute calls are more frequent than calls of any other duration. If daughter's phone call were an activity in a PERT project,
   a. what would be the phone call's expected duration?
   b. what estimate would you give for its variance?
   c. in scheduling the project, how much time would you allocate for the phone call?

4. A small project is composed of seven activities whose time estimates are listed in the table below. Activities are identified by their beginning (i) and ending (j) node numbers.

| Activity | | Estimated duration (weeks) | | |
i	j	Optimistic	Most likely	Pessimistic
1	2	1	1	7
1	3	1	4	7
1	4	2	2	8
2	5	1	1	1
3	5	2	5	14
4	6	2	5	8
5	6	3	6	15

a. Draw the project network and identify all paths through it.
b. Find the expected duration and variance for each activity.
c. Calculate early and late occurrence times for each node. What is the expected project length?
d. Calculate total slack for each activity.

5. In problem 4 calculate the variance and standard deviation of project length. What is the probability that the project will be completed:
a. at least 3 weeks earlier than expected?
b. no more than 3 weeks later than expected?

6. In problem 4 if the project due date is 18 weeks, what is the probability of *not* meeting the due date?

7. In problem 4 what due date has about a 90 per cent chance of being met?

8. The following table lists the jobs of a network along with their time estimates:

| Job | | Duration (days) | | |
i	j	Optimistic	Most likely	Pessimistic
1	2	3	6	15
1	6	2	5	14
2	3	6	12	30
2	4	2	5	8
3	5	5	11	17
4	5	3	6	15
6	7	3	9	27
5	8	1	4	7
7	8	4	19	28

a. Draw the project network.
b. Calculate the length and variance of the critical path.
c. What is the approximate probability that jobs on the critical path will be completed by the due date of 41 days?
d. What is the approximate probability that jobs on the next most critical path will be completed by the due date?
e. What is your estimate of the probability that the entire project will be completed by the due date? Explain.

CHAPTER 5—CPM Problems

1. In the project on page 154, activities are represented by arrows, and the number above each activity is both its identification and its normal duration (in days).
a. Determine the minimum length of the project, and identify the activities on the critical path.

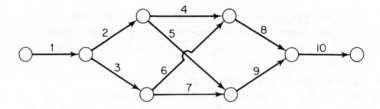

b. Assume that each activity, except 1 and 2, can be shortened up to 2 days at a cost per day equal to the activity number. For example, activity 6 normally takes 6 days but could be shortened to 5 days for a cost of $6, or to 4 days for an additional cost of $6. Determine the least-cost 26-day schedule. Show the new durations of activities which have been shortened and the total cost of shortening the schedule.

2. A small maintenance project consists of the jobs in the table below. With each job is listed its normal time and a minimum, or crash, time (in days). The cost in dollars per day of crashing each job is also given.

Job i	j	Normal days Duration	Minimum (Crash) days Duration	Cost of $/day Crashing
1	2	9	6	20
1	3	8	5	25
1	4	15	10	30
2	4	5	3	10
3	4	10	6	15
4	5	2	1	40

a. What is the normal project length and the minimum project length?

b. Determine the minimum crashing costs of schedules ranging from normal length down to, and including, the minimum length schedule. That is, if L = length of normal schedule, find the costs of schedules which are L, L − 1, L − 2, and so on days long.

c. Overhead costs total $60 per day. What is the optimum length schedule in terms of both crashing and overhead costs? List the scheduled durations of each job for your solution.

3. A maintenance foreman has given the following estimate of times and costs for jobs in a motor overhaul project:

Job		Predecessors	Normal Duration (hours)	Cost $	Minimum Duration	Cost $
A	Remove and disassemble motor	—	8	80	6	100
B	Clean and paint frame	A	7	40	4	94
C	Rewind armature	A	12	100	5	184
D	Replace bearings	A	9	70	5	102
E	Assemble and install motor	B, C, D	6	50	6	50

Assume that the jobs can be done at either normal or fast pace, but not at any pace in between. Plot the relationship between project completion time and minimum total project cost.

4. In problem 3 assume that a linear cost relationship exists between job duration and job cost, and that a job may be scheduled not only at the normal and minimum durations but at any integer duration in between. With overhead costs at $25 an hour, plot the cost-time relationship.

CHAPTER 7—Limited Resource Scheduling

1. The project represented in the table below is to be scheduled within a resource limit of 12 men. All the men are capable of working on any of the jobs. If not assigned on a particular day, a man is idle but still draws pay. Each job must be assigned a crew of men corresponding to one of the three possible crew sizes listed in the table. No in-between assignments may be made, and the crew size must remain fixed for a job until it is finished. Job duration equals man-days divided by crew size for any crew size chosen. Schedule the project so as to minimize idle man-days over its active span.

Job		Resource	Crew Size (men)		
i	j	Requirement (man-days)	Minimum	Normal	Maximum
1	2	32	2	4	8
1	3	48	4	6	8
2	3	40	4	5	8
2	4	12	2	3	4
4	5	30	3	5	6
3	5	54	3	6	9

2. Schedule the project described in the table on page 156, subject to a resource constraint of 16 men. Any man can work on any job. For a given job, any crew size within, and including, the stated limits may be selected, if it is evenly divisible into the resource requirement. (For example, job *b* requires 24 man-days. A crew size of 2, 3, 4 ,or 6 is permissible, but 5 is not.) Crew sizes do not affect efficiency. Schedule length is to be minimized within resource and technological constraints.

3. The problem is the same as in 2 above, with two changes:
   a. Any crew size between the stated limits is permissible (except for fractional assignments). Once a job is started, its crew size must remain fixed; but if the man-days are not evenly divisible by the selected crew

size, the last day scheduled for the job will require fewer than the full crew of men.

b. The overall resource limit may be established anywhere between the limits of 10 and 22 men. Once established, this limit must remain constant over the project schedule period. You are to schedule the project with the least number of idle man-days.

Job	Predecessors	Resource Requirements (man-days)	Range of Permissible Crew Sizes Minimum	Maximum
a	—	45	5	15
b	a	24	2	6
c	a	96	4	12
d	a	50	2	10
e	d	30	2	10
f	c	60	4	12
g	c	12	1	6
h	b	35	5	7
i	f	42	3	14
j	g, e	24	3	8
k	i, j	20	2	10

Answers

Chapter 2

4. a.

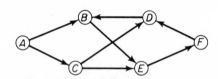

Network contains a cycle (B precedes E, E precedes F, F precedes D, and D precedes B) and redundant arrows (see below).

b.

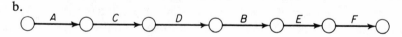

No dummy activities are needed. Note that several redundant predecessor relationships are removed. ("A precedes B" is implied by "A precedes C, C precedes D, and D precedes B." Likewise, "C precedes E" and "D precedes F" are redundant.)

5. a. One possible ordering of activities is shown in the AON diagram:

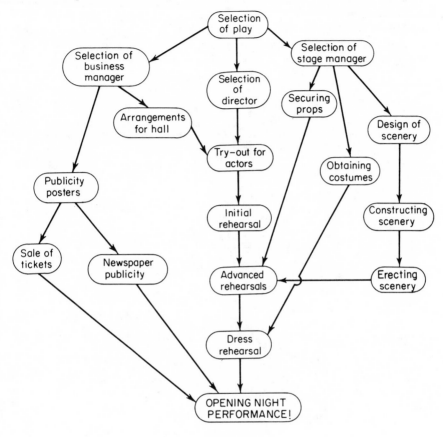

Chapter 3

1. a. and b.

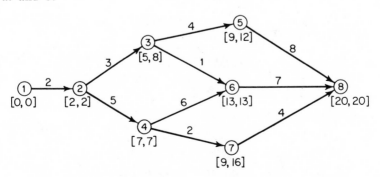

c. 3 days; 0 days; 7 days.
d. (1, 2), (2, 4), (4, 6), (6, 8).
e. Unaffected. Job (2, 3) would become critical, however.
f. Job (3, 6)—7 days; Job (7, 8)—7 days; Job (5, 8)—3 days.
2. a and b.

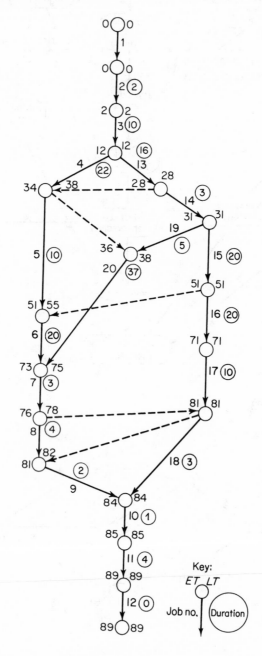

c.

Activity	ES	EF	LS	LF	TS	FS
1	0	0	0	0	0	0
2	0	2	0	2	0	0
3	2	12	2	12	0	0
4	12	34	16	38	4	0
5	34	44	45	55	11	7
6	51	71	55	75	4	2
7	73	76	75	78	2	0
8	76	80	78	82	2	1
9	81	83	82	84	1	1
10	84	85	84	85	0	0
11	85	89	85	89	0	0
12	89	89	89	89	0	0
13	12	28	12	28	0	0
14	28	31	28	31	0	0
15	31	51	31	51	0	0
16	51	71	51	71	0	0
17	71	81	71	81	0	0
18	81	84	81	84	0	0
19	31	36	33	38	2	0
20	36	73	38	75	2	0

d. 1–2–3–13–14–15–16–17–18–10–11–12; 89 minutes.

e. 6 : 01 A.M.

f. 1. no   4. yes
   2. no   5. no
   3. yes   6. no

g. Yes, Mr. Brady has slack in activities 4 through 9. The best time to read the newspaper uninterruptedly would be before or after he gets dressed, when he has 11 minutes slack time. Mrs. Brady must wait until her husband leaves before she can relax with the newspaper.

h.

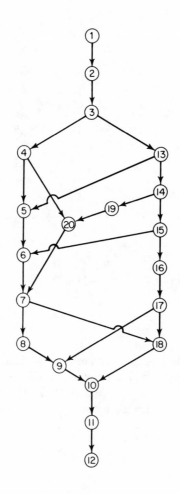

3. a.

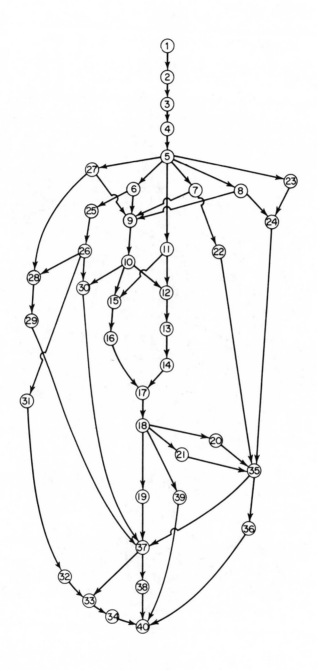

b.

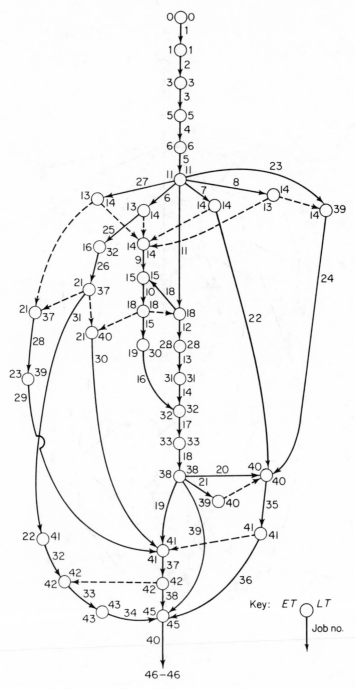

Key: ET ◯ LT

Job no.

162

c.

Job	ES	EF	LS	LF	TS	FS
1	0	1	0	1	0	0
2	1	3	1	3	0	0
3	3	5	3	5	0	0
4	5	6	5	6	0	0
5	6	11	6	11	0	0
6	11	13	12	14	1	0
7	11	14	11	14	0	0
8	11	13	12	14	1	1
9	14	15	14	15	0	0
10	15	18	15	18	0	0
11	11	16	13	18	2	2
12	18	28	18	28	0	0
13	28	31	28	31	0	0
14	31	32	31	32	0	0
15	18	19	29	30	11	0
16	19	21	30	32	11	11
17	32	33	32	33	0	0
18	33	38	33	38	0	0
19	38	40	39	41	1	1
20	38	40	38	40	0	0
21	38	39	39	40	1	1
22	14	15	39	40	25	25
23	11	14	36	39	25	0
24	14	15	39	40	25	25
25	13	16	29	32	16	0
26	16	21	32	37	16	0
27	11	13	12	14	1	1
28	21	23	37	39	16	0
29	23	25	39	41	16	16
30	21	22	40	41	19	19
31	21	22	40	41	19	0
32	22	23	41	42	19	19
33	42	43	42	43	0	0
34	43	45	43	45	0	0
35	40	41	40	41	0	0
36	41	42	44	45	3	3
37	41	42	41	42	0	0
38	42	44	43	45	1	1
39	38	39	44	45	6	6
40	45	46	45	46	0	0

d. 1–2–3–4–5–7–9–10–12–13–14–17–18–20–35–37–33–34–40.
   Minimum length = 46 days.
e. See table in part c.

   f. There are several alternatives, but the following would probably be among the first to be investigated:

     1. Use more carpenters (shorten job 12)

     2. Use more finishers and painters (shorten jobs 13 and 18)

     3. Use more plasterers (shorten job 10)

     4. Use more framers (shorten job 5)

   Shortening the schedule ten days might require simultaneous reduction on parallel critical paths or reconsideration of the technological constraints shown (some may not be "firm" constraints).

   g. If all jobs were started at their early times, the men engaged in activities 6, 7, 8, 11, 23, and 27 (which all begin on day 11) might well get in each other's way. Other examples may also be found.

Chapter 4

1. a. .50 (that is, a 50 per cent chance)

   b. .31

   c. .84

2. About 65 weeks.

3. a. $20\frac{5}{6}$ minutes

   b. Variance $= 84$ (Standard deviation $= 9\frac{1}{6}$ minutes)

   c. $20\frac{5}{6}$ minutes

4. a.

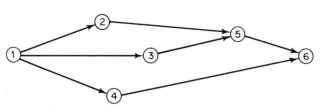

   b.

Activity	Expected Duration (weeks)	Variance
(1,2)	2	1
(1,3)	4	1
(1,4)	3	1
(2,5)	1	0
(3,5)	6	4
(4,6)	5	1
(5,6)	7	4

   c.

Node	ET	LT
1	0	0
2	2	9
3	4	4
4	3	12
5	10	10
6	17	17

Expected project length $= 17$ weeks.

    d. Activities (1, 3), (3, 5), (5, 6):   0 weeks slack
       Activities (1, 2), (2, 5)   :   7 weeks slack
       Activities (1, 4), (4, 6)   :   9 weeks slack

5. Project variance = 9, standard deviation = 3
    a. .16
    b. .84
6. a. About .37
7. About 21 weeks
8. a.

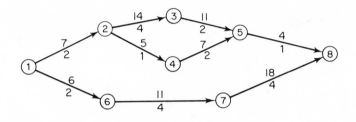

    b. Length = 36 days; variance = 25
    c. .84
    d. .84
    e. About .71. Since the two paths are independent, the probability of their both being completed in 41 days is equal to the product of their separate probabilities of being completed in that time.

Chapter 5

1. a. 30 days; activities 1, 3, 7, 9, 10

b. Activity Changed	New Length (days)	Cost $
3	1	6
7	6	7
9	8	9
	Total	22

2. a. 20 days; 12 days

b.

Length (days)	Crashing Cost $	Total Cost $
20	0	1200
19	15	1155
18	30	1110
17	45	1065
16	85	1045
15	130	1030
14	195	1035
13	260	1040
12	335	1055

c. Optimum length = 15 days (see b.)

Job (1, 2): 9 days
(1, 3): 8 days
(1, 4): 14 days
(2, 4): 5 days
(3, 4): 6 days
(4, 5): 1 day

3.

Project Completion Time (hours)	Minimum Total Cost $	Jobs Shortened
26	340	
25	*	
24	360	A
23	424	C
22	*	
21	444	A and C
20	*	
19	476	A, C, and D
18	*	
17	530	A, B, C, and D

* Cost is the same as next shorter time, with same jobs shortened.

4.

Project Completion Time (hours)	Total Activity Cost $	Total Project Cost $
26	340	990
25	352	977
24	364	964
23	376	951
22	396	946
21	416	941
20	436	936
19	456	931
18	494	944
17	532	957

Chapter 7

1.

Job	Crew Size	Start Time
(1, 2)	8	0
(1, 3)	4	0
(2, 3)	5	4
(2, 4)	3	4
(3, 5)	9	12
(4, 5)	9	12

(Schedule is 18 days long; there are no idle man-days.)

2. One possible solution is as follows:

Job	Crew Size	Start Time
a	15	0
b	4	3
c	6	3
d	5	3
e	5	13
f	10	19
g	6	19
h	5	9
i	14	25
j	6	21
k	10	28

Total length = 30 days.

3. The solution in problem 2 above has 42 idle man-days. Can you find a better solution?

Index